DR. MARTIN LUTHER'S

Small Catechism

A Short Explanation of

DR. MARTIN LUTHER'S

Small
Catechism

A HANDBOOK OF CHRISTIAN DOCTRINE

CONCORDIA PUBLISHING HOUSE

SAINT LOUIS, MISSOURI

SECTION I

The Ten Commandments

AS THE HEAD OF THE FAMILY SHOULD TEACH THEM
IN A SIMPLE WAY TO HIS HOUSEHOLD

—◆—

THE FIRST COMMANDMENT

Thou shalt have no other gods before Me.

What does this mean? We should fear, love, and trust in God above all things.

THE SECOND COMMANDMENT

Thou shalt not take the name of the Lord, thy God, in vain.

What does this mean? We should fear and love God that we may not curse, swear, use witchcraft, lie, or deceive by His name, but call upon it in every trouble, pray, praise, and give thanks.

THE THIRD COMMANDMENT

Remember the Sabbath day, to keep it holy. (Thou shalt sanctify the holy day.)

What does this mean? We should fear and love God that we may not despise preaching and His Word, but hold it sacred and gladly hear and learn it.

THE FOURTH COMMANDMENT

Thou shalt honor thy father and thy mother, that it may be well with thee, and thou mayest live long on the earth.

What does this mean? We should fear and love God that we may not despise our parents and masters, nor provoke them to anger, but give them honor, serve and obey them, and hold them in love and esteem.

THE FIFTH COMMANDMENT

Thou shalt not kill.

What does this mean? We should fear and love God that we may not hurt nor harm our neighbor in his body, but help and befriend him in every bodily need.

THE SIXTH COMMANDMENT

Thou shalt not commit adultery.

What does this mean? We should fear and love God that we may lead a chaste and decent life in word and deed, and each love and honor his spouse.

THE SEVENTH COMMANDMENT

Thou shalt not steal.

What does this mean? We should fear and love God that we may not take our neighbor's money or goods, nor get them by false ware or dealing, but help him to improve and protect his property and business.

THE EIGHTH COMMANDMENT

Thou shalt not bear false witness against thy neighbor.

What does this mean? We should fear and love God that we may not deceitfully belie, betray, slander, nor defame our neighbor, but defend him, speak well of him, and put the best construction on everything.

THE NINTH COMMANDMENT

Thou shalt not covet thy neighbor's house.

What does this mean? We should fear and love God that we may not craftily seek to get our neighbor's inheritance or house, nor obtain it by a show of right, but help and be of service to him in keeping it.

THE TENTH COMMANDMENT

Thou shalt not covet thy neighbor's wife, nor his manservant, nor his maidservant, nor his cattle, nor anything that is thy neighbor's.

What does this mean? We should fear and love God that we may not estrange, force, or entice away from our neighbor his wife, servants, or cattle, but urge them to stay and do their duty.

THE CLOSE OF THE COMMANDMENTS

What does God say of all these Command-ments? He says thus: I, the Lord, thy God, am a jealous God, visiting the iniquity of the fathers upon the children unto the third and fourth generation of them that hate Me, and showing mercy unto thousands of them that love Me and keep My Commandments.

What does this mean? God threatens to punish all that transgress these Commandments. Therefore we should fear His wrath and not act contrary to them. But He promises grace and every blessing to all that keep these Command-ments. Therefore we should also love and trust in Him and willingly do according to His Com-mandments.

The Creed

AS THE HEAD OF THE FAMILY SHOULD TEACH IT
IN A SIMPLE WAY TO HIS HOUSEHOLD

---◆---

THE FIRST ARTICLE

CREATION

I believe in God the Father Almighty, Maker of heaven and earth.

What does this mean? I believe that God has made me and all creatures; that He has given me my body and soul, eyes, ears, and all my members, my reason and all my senses, and still preserves them;

also clothing and shoes, meat and drink, house and home, wife and children, fields, cattle, and all my goods; that He richly and daily provides me with all that I need to support this body and life;

that He defends me against all danger, and guards and protects me from all evil;

and all this purely out of fatherly, divine goodness and mercy, without any merit or worthiness in me;

for all which it is my duty to thank and praise, to serve and obey Him.

This is most certainly true.

THE SECOND ARTICLE

REDEMPTION

And in Jesus Christ, His only Son, our Lord, who was conceived by the Holy Ghost, born of the Virgin Mary, suffered under Pontius Pilate, was crucified, dead, and buried;

He descended into hell; the third day He rose again from the dead; He ascended into heaven, and sitteth on the right hand of God the Father Almighty; from thence He shall come to judge the quick and the dead.

What does this mean? I believe that Jesus Christ, true God, begotten of the Father from eternity, and also true man, born of the Virgin Mary, is my Lord,

who has redeemed me, a lost and condemned creature, purchased and won me from all sins, from death, and from the power of the devil; not with gold or silver, but with His holy, precious blood and with His innocent suffering and death,

that I may be His own, and live under Him in His kingdom, and serve Him in everlasting righteousness, innocence, and blessedness,

even as He is risen from the dead, lives and reigns to all eternity.

This is most certainly true.

THE THIRD ARTICLE

SANCTIFICATION

I believe in the Holy Ghost; the holy Christian Church, the communion of saints; the forgiveness of sins; the resurrection of the body; and the life everlasting. Amen.

What does this mean? I believe that I cannot by my own reason or strength believe in Jesus Christ, my Lord, or come to Him; but the Holy Ghost has called me by the Gospel, enlightened me with His gifts, sanctified and kept me in the true faith;

even as He calls, gathers, enlightens, and sanctifies the whole Christian Church on earth, and keeps it with Jesus Christ in the one true faith;

in which Christian Church He daily and richly forgives all sins to me and all believers,

and will at the Last Day raise up me and all the dead, and give unto me and all believers in Christ eternal life.

This is most certainly true.

The Lord's Prayer

AS THE HEAD OF THE FAMILY SHOULD TEACH IT
IN A SIMPLE WAY TO HIS HOUSEHOLD

—◆—

Our Father who art in heaven. Hallowed
be Thy name. Thy kingdom come. Thy will
be done on earth as it is in heaven. Give us
this day our daily bread. And forgive us our
trespasses, as we forgive those who trespass
against us. And lead us not into temptation, but
deliver us from evil. For Thine is the kingdom
and the power and the glory forever and ever.
Amen.

THE INTRODUCTION

Our Father who art in heaven.

What does this mean? God would by these
words tenderly invite us to believe that He is
our true Father, and that we are His true children, so that we may with all boldness and confidence ask Him as dear children ask their dear
father.

THE FIRST PETITION

Hallowed be Thy name.

What does this mean? God's name is indeed
holy in itself; but we pray in this petition that it
may be holy among us also.

How is this done? When the Word of God
is taught in its truth and purity, and we, as the

children of God, also lead a holy life according to it. This grant us, dear Father in heaven. But he that teaches and lives otherwise than God's Word teaches, profanes the name of God among us. From this preserve us, Heavenly Father.

THE SECOND PETITION

Thy kingdom come.

What does this mean? The kingdom of God comes indeed without our prayer, of itself; but we pray in this petition that it may come unto us also.

How is this done? When our heavenly Father gives us His Holy Spirit, so that by His grace we believe His holy Word and lead a godly life, here in time and hereafter in eternity.

THE THIRD PETITION

Thy will be done on earth as it is in heaven.

What does this mean? The good and gracious will of God is done indeed without our prayer; but we pray in this petition that it may be done among us also.

How is this done? When God breaks and hinders every evil counsel and will which would not let us hallow God's name nor let His kingdom come, such as the will of the devil, the world, and our flesh; but strengthens and preserves us steadfast in His Word and faith unto our end. This is His gracious and good will.

THE FOURTH PETITION

Give us this day our daily bread.

What does this mean? God gives daily bread indeed without our prayer, also to all the wicked; but we pray in this petition that He would lead us to know it, and to receive our daily bread with thanksgiving.

What is meant by daily bread? Everything that belongs to the support and wants of the body, such as food, drink, clothing, shoes, house, home, field, cattle, money, goods, a pious spouse, pious children, pious servants, pious and faithful rulers, good government, good weather, peace, health, discipline, honor, good friends, faithful neighbors, and the like.

THE FIFTH PETITION

And forgive us our trespasses, as we forgive those who trespass against us.

What does this mean? We pray in this petition that our Father in heaven would not look upon our sins, nor on their account deny our prayer; for we are worthy of none of the things for which we pray, neither have we deserved them; but that He would grant them all to us by grace; for we daily sin much and indeed deserve nothing but punishment. So will we also heartily forgive, and readily do good to, those who sin against us.

THE SIXTH PETITION

And lead us not into temptation.

What does this mean? God indeed tempts no one; but we pray in this petition that God would guard and keep us, so that the devil, the world, and our flesh may not deceive us nor seduce us into misbelief, despair, and other great shame and vice; and though we be assailed by them, that still we may finally overcome and obtain the victory.

THE SEVENTH PETITION

But deliver us from evil.

What does this mean? We pray in this petition, as the sum of all, that our Father in heaven would deliver us from every evil of body and soul, property and honor, and finally, when our last hour has come, grant us a blessed end, and graciously take us from this vale of tears to Himself in heaven.

THE CONCLUSION

For Thine is the kingdom and the power and the glory forever and ever. Amen.

What is meant by the word "Amen"? That I should be certain that these petitions are acceptable to our Father in heaven, and are heard by Him; for He Himself has commanded us so to pray, and has promised to hear us. Amen, Amen, that is, Yea, yea, it shall be so.

The Sacrament of Holy Baptism

AS THE HEAD OF THE FAMILY SHOULD TEACH IT
IN A SIMPLE WAY TO HIS HOUSEHOLD

—⋄—

I. THE NATURE OF BAPTISM

What is Baptism?

Baptism is not simple water only, but it is
the water comprehended in God's command and
connected with God's word.

Which is that word of God?

Christ, our Lord, says in the last chapter of
Matthew: Go ye and teach all nations, baptizing
them in the name of the Father and of the Son
and of the Holy Ghost.

II. THE BLESSINGS OF BAPTISM

What does Baptism give or profit?

It works forgiveness of sins, delivers from
death and the devil, and gives eternal salvation
to all who believe this, as the words and promises
of God declare

Which are such words and promises of God?

Christ, our Lord, says in the last chapter of
Mark: He that believeth and is baptized shall
be saved; but he that believeth not shall be
damned.

III. THE POWER OF BAPTISM

How can water do such great things?

It is not the water indeed that does them, but the word of God which is in and with the water, and faith, which trusts such word of God in the water. For without the word of God the water is simple water and no Baptism. But with the word of God it is a Baptism, that is, a gracious water of life and a washing of regeneration in the Holy Ghost, as St. Paul says, Titus, chapter third:

[According to His mercy He saved us] By the washing of regeneration and renewing of the Holy Ghost, which He shed on us abundantly through Jesus Christ, our Savior, that, being justified by His grace, we should be made heirs according to the hope of eternal life. This is a faithful saying.

IV. THE SIGNIFICANCE OF BAPTIZING WITH WATER

What does such baptizing with water signify?

It signifies that the Old Adam in us should, by daily contrition and repentance, be drowned and die with all sins and evil lusts and, again, a new man daily come forth and arise, who shall live before God in righteousness and purity forever.

Where is this written?

St. Paul writes, Romans, chapter sixth: We are buried with Christ by Baptism into death, that, like as He was raised up from the dead by the glory of the Father, even so we also should walk in newness of life.

The Office of the Keys and Confession

AS THE HEAD OF THE FAMILY SHOULD TEACH IT
IN A SIMPLE WAY TO HIS HOUSEHOLD

—◇—

What is the Office of the Keys?

It is the peculiar church power which Christ has given to His Church on earth to forgive the sins of penitent sinners, but to retain the sins of the impenitent as long as they do not repent.

Where is this written?

Thus writes the holy Evangelist John, chapter twentieth:

The Lord Jesus breathed on His disciples and saith unto them, Receive ye the Holy Ghost. Whosoever sins ye remit, they are remitted unto them; and whosoever sins ye retain, they are retained.

What do you believe according to these words?

I believe that, when the called ministers of Christ deal with us by His divine command, especially when they exclude manifest and impenitent sinners from the Christian congregation, and, again, when they absolve those who repent of their sins and are willing to amend, this is as valid and certain, in heaven also, as if Christ, our dear Lord, dealt with us Himself.

What is Confession?

Confession embraces two parts. One is that we confess our sins; the other, that we receive absolution, or forgiveness, from the pastor as from God Himself, and in no wise doubt, but firmly believe, that by it our sins are forgiven before God in heaven.

What sins should we confess?

Before God we should plead guilty of all sins, even of those which we do not know, as we do in the Lord's Prayer; but before the pastor we should confess those sins only which we know and feel in our hearts.

Which are these?

Here consider your station according to the Ten Commandments, whether you are a father, mother, son, daughter, master, mistress, servant; whether you have been disobedient, unfaithful, slothful; whether you have grieved any person by word or deed; whether you have stolen, neglected, or wasted aught, or done other injury.

The Sacrament of the Altar

AS THE HEAD OF THE FAMILY SHOULD TEACH IT
IN A SIMPLE WAY TO HIS HOUSEHOLD

—◇—

What is the Sacrament of the Altar?

It is the true body and blood of our Lord Jesus Christ under the bread and wine, for us Christians to eat and to drink, instituted by Christ Himself.

Where is this written?

The holy Evangelists Matthew, Mark, Luke, and St. Paul [the Apostle] write thus:

Our Lord Jesus Christ, the same night in which He was betrayed, took bread; and when He had given thanks, He brake it and gave it to His disciples, saying, Take, eat; this is My body, which is given for you. This do in remembrance of Me.

After the same manner also He took the cup when He had supped, and when He had given thanks, He gave it to them, saying, Drink ye all of it; this cup is the new testament in My blood, which is shed for you for the remission of sins. This do, as oft as ye drink it, in remembrance of Me.

What is the benefit of such eating and drinking?

That is shown us by these words, "Given and shed for you for the remission of sins"; namely, that in the Sacrament forgiveness of sins, life, and salvation are given us through these words. For where there is forgiveness of sins, there is also life and salvation.

How can bodily eating and drinking do such great things?

It is not the eating and drinking indeed that does them, but the words here written, "Given and shed for you for the remission of sins"; which words, besides the bodily eating and drinking, are the chief thing in the Sacrament; and he that believes these words has what they say and express, namely, the forgiveness of sins.

Who, then, receives such Sacrament worthily?

Fasting and bodily preparation are indeed a fine outward training; but he is truly worthy and well prepared who has faith in these words, "Given and shed for you for the remission of sins."

But he that does not believe these words, or doubts, is unworthy and unprepared; for the words "for you" require all hearts to believe.

SECTION II

How the Head of the Family Should Teach His Household to Pray Morning and Evening

MORNING PRAYER

In the morning, when you get up, make the sign of the holy cross and say:

In the name of ✠ the Father and of the Son and of the Holy Ghost. Amen.

Then, kneeling or standing, repeat the Creed and the Lord's Prayer. If you choose, you may also say this little prayer:

I thank Thee, my heavenly Father, through Jesus Christ, Thy dear Son, that Thou hast kept me this night from all harm and danger; and I pray Thee that Thou wouldst keep me this day also from sin and every evil, that all my doings and life may please Thee. For into Thy hands I commend myself, my body and soul, and all things. Let Thy holy angel be with me, that the wicked Foe may have no power over me. Amen.

Then go joyfully to your work, singing a hymn, like that of the Ten Commandments, or whatever your devotion may suggest.

EVENING PRAYER

In the evening, when you go to bed, make the sign of the holy cross and say:

In the name of ✠ the Father and of the Son and of the Holy Ghost. Amen.

Then, kneeling or standing, repeat the Creed and the Lord's Prayer. If you choose, you may also say this little prayer:

I thank Thee, my heavenly Father, through Jesus Christ, Thy dear Son, that Thou hast graciously kept me this day; and I pray Thee that Thou wouldst forgive me all my sins where I have done wrong, and graciously keep me this night. For into Thy hands I commend myself, my body and soul, and all things. Let Thy holy angel be with me, that the wicked Foe may have no power over me. Amen.

Then go to sleep at once and in good cheer.

How the Head of the Family Should Teach His Household to Ask a Blessing and Return Thanks

ASKING A BLESSING

The children and members of the household shall go to the table reverently, fold their hands, and say:

The eyes of all wait upon Thee, O Lord, and Thou givest them their meat in due season; Thou openest Thine hand and satisfiest the desire of every living thing.

Then shall be said the Lord's Prayer and the following:

Lord God, Heavenly Father, bless us and these Thy gifts which we receive from Thy bountiful goodness, through Jesus Christ, our Lord. Amen.

RETURNING THANKS

Also, after eating, they shall, in like manner, reverently and with folded hands say:

Oh, give thanks unto the Lord, for He is good, for His mercy endureth forever. He giveth food to all flesh; He giveth to the beast his food, and to the young ravens which cry. He delighteth not in the strength of the horse. He taketh not pleasure in the legs of a man. The Lord taketh pleasure in them that fear Him, in those that hope in His mercy.

Then shall be said the Lord's Prayer. and the following:

We thank Thee, Lord God, Heavenly Father, through Jesus Christ, our Lord, for all Thy benefits, who livest and reignest forever and ever. Amen.

SECTION III

Table of Duties

OR CERTAIN PASSAGES OF SCRIPTURE FOR VARIOUS
HOLY ORDERS AND ESTATES WHEREBY THESE ARE
SEVERALLY TO BE ADMONISHED AS TO THEIR OFFICE
AND DUTY

—◆—

TO BISHOPS, PASTORS, AND PREACHERS

A bishop must be blameless, the husband of
one wife, vigilant, sober, of good behavior, given
to hospitality, apt to teach; not given to wine,
no striker, not greedy of filthy lucre; but patient,
not a brawler, not covetous; one that ruleth well
his own house, having his children in subjection
with all gravity; not a novice; holding fast the
faithful Word as he hath been taught, that he
may be able by sound doctrine both to exhort
and to convince the gainsayers. *1 Tim. 3:2, 3,
4, 6; Titus 1:9.*

WHAT THE HEARERS OWE TO THEIR PASTORS

Eat and drink such things as they give; for
the laborer is worthy of his hire. *Luke 10:7.*

Even so hath the Lord ordained that they
which preach the Gospel should live of the
Gospel. *1 Cor. 9:14.*

Let him that is taught in the Word communicate unto him that teacheth in all good
things. Be not deceived; God is not mocked;

for whatsoever a man soweth, that shall he also reap. *Gal. 6:6, 7.*

Let the elders that rule well be counted worthy of double honor, especially they who labor in the Word and doctrine. For the Scripture saith, Thou shalt not muzzle the ox that treadeth out the corn; and, The laborer is worthy of his reward. *1 Tim. 5:17, 18.*

And we beseech you, brethren, to know them which labor among you and are over you in the Lord and admonish you; and to esteem them very highly in love for their work's sake. And be at peace among yourselves. *1 Thess. 5:12, 13.*

Obey them that have the rule over you, and submit yourselves; for they watch for your souls as they that must give account, that they may do it with joy and not with grief; for that is unprofitable for you. *Heb. 13:17.*

OF CIVIL GOVERNMENT

Let every soul be subject unto the higher powers. For there is no power but of God; the powers that be are ordained of God. Whosoever therefore resisteth the power, resisteth the ordinance of God; and they that resist shall receive to themselves damnation. For rulers are not a terror to good works, but to the evil. Wilt thou, then, not be afraid of the power? Do that which is good, and thou shalt have praise of the same; for he is the minister of God to thee for good. But if thou do that which is evil, be afraid, for he beareth not the sword in vain; for he is the minister of God, a revenger to execute wrath upon him that doeth evil. *Rom. 13:1-4.*

OF SUBJECTS

Render unto Caesar the things which are Caesar's, and unto God the things that are God's. *Matt. 22:21.*

Wherefore ye must needs be subject, not only for wrath, but also for conscience' sake. For, for this cause pay ye tribute also; for they are God's ministers, attending continually upon this very thing. Render therefore to all their dues: tribute to whom tribute is due; custom, to whom custom; fear, to whom fear; honor, to whom honor. *Rom. 13:5-7.*

I exhort therefore that, first of all, supplications, prayers, intercessions, and giving of thanks be made for all men, for kings, and for all that are in authority, that we may lead a quiet and peaceable life in all godliness and honesty. For this is good and acceptable in the sight of God, our Savior. *1 Tim. 2:1-3.*

Put them in mind to be subject to principalities and powers, to obey magistrates, to be ready to every good work. *Titus 3:1.*

Submit yourselves to every ordinance of man for the Lord's sake: whether it be to the king, as supreme; or unto governors, as unto them that are sent by him for the punishment of evildoers, and for the praise of them that do well. *1 Peter 2:13, 14.*

TO HUSBANDS

Likewise, ye husbands, dwell with them according to knowledge, giving honor unto the wife, as unto the weaker vessel, and as being heirs together of the grace of life, that your prayers be not hindered. And be not bitter against them. *1 Peter 3:7; Col. 3:19.*

TO WIVES

Wives, submit yourselves unto your own husbands as unto the Lord. *Eph. 5:22.*

Even as Sarah obeyed Abraham, calling him lord; whose daughters ye are, as long as ye do well, and are not afraid with any amazement. *1 Peter 3:6.*

TO PARENTS

And, ye fathers, provoke not your children to wrath, but bring them up in the nurture and admonition of the Lord. *Eph. 6:4.*

TO CHILDREN

Children, obey your parents in the Lord; for this is right. Honor thy father and mother; which is the first commandment with promise: that it may be well with thee, and thou mayest live long on the earth. *Eph. 6:1-3.*

TO SERVANTS, HIRED MEN, AND EMPLOYEES

Servants, be obedient to them that are your masters according to the flesh, with fear and trembling, in singleness of your heart, as unto Christ; not with eyeservice, as men-pleasers, but as the servants of Christ, doing the will of God from the heart; with good will doing service as to the Lord, and not to men; knowing that whatsoever good thing any man doeth, the same shall he receive of the Lord, whether he be bond or free. *Eph.* 6:5-8.

TO EMPLOYERS

And, ye masters, do the same things unto them, forbearing threatening, knowing that your Master also is in heaven; neither is there respect of persons with Him. *Eph.* 6:9.

TO THE YOUNG IN GENERAL

Likewise, ye younger, submit yourselves unto the elder. Yea, all of you be subject one to another, and be clothed with humility; for God resisteth the proud and giveth grace to the humble. Humble yourselves therefore under the mighty hand of God, that He may exalt you in due time. *1 Peter* 5:5, 6.

TO WIDOWS

Now, she that is a widow indeed, and deso-late, trusteth in God, and continueth in supplications and prayers night and day. But she that liveth in pleasure is dead while she liveth. *1 Tim. 5:5, 6.*

TO ALL IN COMMON

Thou shalt love thy neighbor as thyself. Herein are comprehended all the Commandments. *Rom. 13:9.* And persevere in prayer for all men. *1 Tim. 2:1.*

> *Let each his lesson learn with care,*
> *And all the household well shall fare.*

SECTION IV

Christian Questions with Their Answers

DRAWN UP BY DR. MARTIN LUTHER FOR THOSE WHO
INTEND TO GO TO THE SACRAMENT

—◆—

After Confession and instruction in the Ten Commandments, the Creed, the Lord's Prayer, and the Sacraments of Baptism and the Holy Supper, the pastor may ask, or one may ask himself:

1. Do you believe that you are a sinner?

Yes, I believe it; I am a sinner.

2. How do you know this?

From the Ten Commandments; these I have not kept.

3. Are you also sorry for your sins?

Yes, I am sorry that I have sinned against God.

4. What have you deserved of God by your sins?

His wrath and displeasure, temporal death, and eternal damnation. Rom. 6:21, 23.

5. Do you also hope to be saved?

Yes, such is my hope.

6. In whom, then, do you trust?

In my dear Lord Jesus Christ.

7. Who is Christ?

The Son of God, true God and man.

8. How many Gods are there?

Only one; but there are three Persons: Father, Son, and Holy Ghost.

9. What, then, has Christ done for you that you trust in Him?

He died for me and shed His blood for me on the cross for the forgiveness of sins.

10. Did the Father also die for you?

He did not; for the Father is God only, the Holy Ghost likewise; but the Son is true God and true man; He died for me and shed His blood for me.

11. How do you know this?

From the holy Gospel and from the words of the Sacrament, and by His body and blood given me as a pledge in the Sacrament.

12. How do those words read?

Our Lord Jesus Christ, the same night in which He was betrayed, took bread; and when He had given thanks, He brake it and gave it to His disciples, saying, Take, eat; this is My body, which is given for you. This do in remembrance of Me.

After the same manner also He took the cup when He had supped, and when He had given thanks, He gave it to them, saying, Drink ye all of it; this cup is the new testament in My blood, which is shed for you for the remission of sins. This do, as oft as ye drink it, in remembrance of Me.

13. You believe, then, that the true body and blood of Christ are in the Sacrament?

Yes, I believe it.

14. What induces you to believe this?

The word of Christ, Take, eat, this is My body; Drink ye all of it, this is My blood.

15. What ought we to do when we eat His body and drink His blood, and thus receive the pledge?

We ought to remember and proclaim His death and the shedding of His blood, as He taught us: This do, as oft as ye drink it, in remembrance of Me.

16. Why ought we to remember and proclaim His death?

That we may learn to believe that no creature could make satisfaction for our sins but Christ, true God and man; and that we may learn to look with terror at our sins, and to regard them as great indeed, and to find joy and comfort in Him alone, and thus be saved through such faith.

17. What was it that moved Him to die and make satisfaction for your sins?

His great love to His Father and to me and other sinners, as it is written in John 14; Rom. 5; Gal. 2; Eph. 5.

18. Finally, why do you wish to go to the Sacrament?

That I may learn to believe that Christ died for *my* sin out of great love, as before said; and that I may also learn of Him to love God and my neighbor.

19. What should admonish and incite a Christian to receive the Sacrament frequently?

In respect to God, both the command and the promise of Christ the Lord should move him, and in respect to himself, the trouble that lies heavy on him, on account of which such command, encouragement, and promise are given.

20. But what shall a person do if he be not sensible of such trouble and feel no hunger and thirst for the Sacrament?

To such a person no better advice can be given than that, in the first place, he put his hand into his bosom, and feel whether he still have flesh and blood, and that he by all means believe what the Scriptures say of it in Gal. 5 and Rom. 7.

Secondly, that he look around to see whether he is still in the world, and keep in mind that there will be no lack of sin and trouble, as the Scriptures say in John 15 and 16; 1 John 2 and 5.

Thirdly, he will certainly have the devil also about him, who with his lying and murdering, day and night, will let him have no peace within or without, as the Scriptures picture him in John 8 and 16; 1 Peter 5; Eph. 6; 2 Tim. 2.

NOTE

These questions and answers are no child's play, but are drawn up with great earnestness of purpose by the venerable and pious Dr. Luther for both young and old. Let each one take heed and likewise consider it a serious matter; for St. Paul writes to the Galatians, chapter sixth: "Be not deceived; God is not mocked."

A SHORT EXPLANATION

OF DR. MARTIN LUTHER'S

SMALL CATECHISM

INTRODUCTION

—◇—

1. What do we call the book which we are about to study?

We call this book "The Catechism."

2. What is a catechism?

A catechism is a book of instruction in the form of questions and answers.

3. Who wrote our Small Catechism?

Doctor Martin Luther wrote our Small Catechism. (1529 A. D.)

4. What does Luther's Small Catechism contain?

Luther's Small Catechism contains *the chief parts of Christian doctrine.*

5. Which are the chief parts of Christian doctrine?

1. The Ten Commandments.
2. The Apostles' Creed.
3. The Lord's Prayer.
4. The Sacrament of Holy Baptism.
5. The Office of the Keys and Confession.
6. The Sacrament of the Altar.

6. From which book did Luther take these chief parts of Christian doctrine?

Luther took the chief parts of Christian doctrine *from the Bible.*

The Bible

7. What is the Bible?

The Bible is the *Word of God.*

NOTE. — Other names for the Bible are: Holy Scripture, The Scriptures, Holy Writ, The Book of Books, The Word of God.

8. Who wrote the Bible?

Holy men of God wrote the Bible. The *Prophets* wrote the books of the Old Testament, and the *Evangelists* and the *Apostles* wrote the books of the New Testament.

NOTE. — For the books of the Bible see page 209.

1   *Holy men of God* spake as they were moved by the Holy Ghost. *2 Peter 1:21.*

9. Why is the Bible the Word of God although it was written by men?

The Bible is the Word of God because these men wrote it *by inspiration of God.*

2   All Scripture is given *by inspiration of God. 2 Tim. 3:16.*

10. What does "by inspiration of God" mean?

"By inspiration of God" means that God the Holy Ghost *moved* the holy men *to write*, and *put into their minds*, the very *thoughts* which they expressed and the very *words* which they wrote. (Verbal Inspiration.)

3   Holy men of God spake as they were *moved by the Holy Ghost. 2 Peter 1:21.*

4   We speak, not in *the words* which man's wisdom teacheth, but *which the Holy Ghost teacheth. 1 Cor. 2:13.*

11. Whose word, then, is every word of the Bible?

Every word of the Bible is *God's word*, and therefore the Bible is without error.

5   Thy Word is *truth. John 17:17.*

6   *All Scripture* is given by inspiration of God. *2 Tim. 3:16.*

7   The Scripture *cannot be broken. John 10:35.*

12. For what purpose did God give us the Bible?

God gave us the Bible to make us *"wise unto salvation* through faith which is in Christ Jesus," and to *train us in holy living*.

8   From a child thou hast known the Holy Scriptures, which are able to *make thee wise unto salvation through faith which is in Christ Jesus.* All Scripture is given by inspiration of God and is profitable *for doctrine, for reproof, for correction, for instruction in righteousness*, that the man of God may be perfect, thoroughly furnished *unto all good works. 2 Tim. 3:15-17.*

9   Thy Word is a *lamp unto my feet* and a *light unto my path. Ps. 119:105.*

13. What use should we make of the Bible?

We should diligently and reverently *read and study* the Bible, *listen* attentively when it is read and explained, *believe* it, and *live* according to it.

10   *Search the Scriptures;* for in them ye think ye have eternal life; and they are they which testify of Me. *John 5:39.*

11   Blessed are they that *hear* the Word of God and *keep* it. *Luke 11:28.*

12   Mary *kept* all these things and *pondered* them in her heart. *Luke 2:19.*

13   If a man love Me, he will *keep My words. John 14:23.*

Law and Gospel

14. What are the two great doctrines of the Bible?

Law and Gospel are the two great doctrines of the Bible.

15. What is the Law?

The Law is that doctrine of the Bible in which God tells us how we *are to be* and what we *are to do* and *not to do.*

Scroll of the Law

14   Ye shall *be holy;* for I, the Lord, your God, am holy. *Lev. 19:2.*

15   *Observe* thou that which I command thee. *Ex. 34:11.*

16   These words which *I command thee* this day shall be in thine heart; and *thou shalt* teach them diligently unto thy children. *Deut. 6:6, 7.*

16. What is the Gospel?

The Gospel is that doctrine of the Bible in which God tells us the good news of our salvation in Jesus Christ.

17   In this was manifested the *love of God* toward us, because that God *sent His only-begotten Son* into the world that we might *live through Him. 1 John 4:9.*

18   God so loved the world that He *gave His only-begotten Son,* that *whosoever believeth in Him* should not perish, but *have everlasting life. John 3:16.*

19   I am not ashamed of the *Gospel of Christ;* for it is the *power of God unto salvation. Rom. 1:16.*

17. What is the difference between the Law and the Gospel?

1. The Law teaches what *we* are to do and not to do; the Gospel teaches what *God* has done, and still does, for our salvation.

2. The Law shows us *our sin* and the *wrath of God;* the Gospel shows us *our Savior* and the *grace of God.*

3. The Law must be preached to all men, but especially to *impenitent* sinners; the Gospel must be preached to sinners who are *troubled* in their minds because of their sins.

PART I

The Ten Commandments

18. What are the Ten Commandments?

The Ten Commandments are the *Law of God*.

NOTE. — The Lord gave the Ten Commandments, but He did not say which is the First, the Second, the Third, etc. Not all churches use the same order in numbering the Commandments.

19. How did God give His Law?

When God created man, He *wrote* the Law *into man's heart*. Later He arranged the Law in Ten Commandments, wrote it *on two tables of stone,* and made it known through Moses.

20   When the Gentiles, which have not the Law, do by nature the things contained in the Law, these, having not the Law, are a law unto themselves: which show the work of *the Law written in their hearts,* their conscience also bearing witness, and their thoughts the meanwhile accusing or else excusing one another. *Rom. 2:14, 15.*

Bible Narrative: There are three kinds of laws in the Old Testament: the *Moral Law,* which tells all men their duty towards God and man; the *Ceremonial Law,* which regulated the religious practices of the Jews in the Old Testament; and the *Political Law,* which was the state law of the Jews. — Only the *Moral Law* was written into man's heart. *Ex. 19 and 20.*

44

20. What is the summary of the First Table of the Law? (Commandments 1—3.)

"Thou shalt *love the Lord,* thy God, with all thy heart and with all thy soul and with all thy mind." *Matt. 22:37.*

21. What is the summary of the Second Table? (Commandments 4—10.)

"Thou shalt *love thy neighbor* as thyself." *Matt. 22:39.*

22. What is the summary of all the Commandments?

Love is the summary of all the Commandments.

21   *Love is the fulfilling* of the Law. *Rom. 13:10.*

23. Whom does God mean when in the Ten Commandments He says, "Thou shalt"?

He means *me* and *all other human beings.*

THE FIRST TABLE

THE FIRST COMMANDMENT

GOD

Thou shalt have no other gods before Me.

What does this mean? We should fear, love, and trust in God above all things.

24. How do you know that there is a God?

I know that there is a God —

A. From the *existence of the world*. (Natural knowledge of God.)

22   Every house is builded by some man; but *He that built all things is God. Heb. 3:4.*

23   The *heavens declare* the glory of God, and *the firmament showeth* His handiwork. *Ps. 19:1.*

24   That which may be known of God is manifest in them [the Gentiles]; for God hath showed it unto them. For the invisible things of Him from the creation of the world *are clearly seen, being understood by the things that are made,* even His eternal power and Godhead, so that they are *without excuse. Rom. 1:19, 20.*

B. From the *testimony of my conscience.* (Natural knowledge of God.)

25   [The Gentiles] show the work of the Law written in their hearts, their *conscience* also bearing witness, and their thoughts the meanwhile accusing or else excusing one another. *Rom. 2:15.*

C. *Especially from the Holy Scriptures*, in which God *clearly* reveals Himself to us. (Revealed knowledge of God.)

26   I am the Lord; that is My name. *Is. 42:8.*

27   The Lord is the *true God*, He is the *living God* and an everlasting King. *Jer. 10:10.*

28   This is life eternal, that they might know Thee the *only true God*, and Jesus Christ, whom Thou hast sent. *John 17:3.*

NOTE. — See Acts 17:23, 24.

25. What is God?

"God is a spirit." John 4:24. (A being endowed with mind and will but without a body. Luke 24:39.)

God is —

A. *Eternal* (without beginning and without end);

29   Lord, Thou hast been our Dwelling Place in all generations. Before the mountains were brought forth or ever Thou hadst formed the earth and the world, even *from everlasting to everlasting*, Thou art, God. Ps. 90:1, 2.

Never-Ending Circle

B. *Unchangeable;*

30   I am the Lord, *I change not. Mal.* 3:6.

31   Thou art *the same,* and Thy years shall have no end. Ps. 102:27.

C. *Omnipotent* (almighty, all-powerful);

32   I am the *almighty* God. *Gen.* 17:1.

33   With God *nothing* shall be *impossible. Luke* 1:37.

34   With God *all things are possible. Matt.* 19:26.

D. *Omniscient* (all-knowing);

35   O Lord, Thou hast searched me and *known me,* Thou *knowest my downsitting* and mine *uprising,* Thou understandest my *thought afar off.* Thou compassest my path and my lying down and *art acquainted* with *all my ways.* For there is not a word in my tongue but, lo, O Lord, *Thou knowest it altogether.* Ps. 139:1-4.

The All-Seeing Eye

36   Lord, Thou *knowest all things. John* 21:17.

E. *Omnipresent* (present everywhere);

37   Can any hide himself in secret places that I shall not see him? saith the Lord. Do not I *fill heaven and earth?* saith the Lord. *Jer. 23:24.*

F. *Holy* (sinless and hating sin);

38   I, the Lord, your God, am *holy. Lev. 19:2.*

39   *Holy, holy, holy,* is the Lord of hosts. *Is. 6:3.*

G. *Just* (fair and impartial);

40   A God of truth and without iniquity, *just* and right is He. *Deut. 32:4.*

H. *Faithful* (keeping His promises);

41   He abideth *faithful;* He cannot deny Himself. *2 Tim. 2:13.*

I. *Benevolent* (good, kind, desiring our welfare);

42   The Lord is *good* to all, and His tender mercies are over all His works. *Ps. 145:9.*

J. *Merciful* (full of pity);

43   His tender *mercies* are over all His works. *Ps. 145:9.*

K. *Gracious* (showing undeserved kindness, forgiving).

44   The Lord, the Lord God, merciful and *gracious,* long-suffering, and abundant in goodness and truth, keeping mercy for thousands, *forgiving iniquity and transgression and sin. Ex. 34:6, 7.*

45   God is *Love. 1 John 4:8.*

NOTE. — Eternity, unchangeableness, omnipotence, omniscience, omnipresence, holiness, etc., are *attributes* of God.

Trinity in Unity
Unity in Trinity

26. Who is the only true God?

The only true God is the *Triune God:* Father, Son, and Holy Ghost, three distinct Persons in one divine Being, or Essence. (The Holy Trinity.)

46   Hear, O Israel: The Lord, our God, is *one* Lord. *Deut. 6:4.*

47   There is none other God but *one. 1 Cor. 8:4.*

48   Go ye therefore and teach all nations, baptizing them in the name of the *Father* and of the *Son* and of the *Holy Ghost. Matt. 28:19.*

49   The grace of the Lord *Jesus Christ* and the love of *God* and the communion of the *Holy Ghost* be with you all. *2 Cor. 13:14.*

50   The *Lord* bless thee and keep thee; the *Lord* make His face shine upon thee and be gracious unto thee; the *Lord* lift up His countenance upon thee and give thee peace. *Num. 6:24-26.*

Bible Narrative: At His baptism Jesus stood in the Jordan; the Father spoke from heaven; the Spirit of God descended upon Jesus in the form of a dove. *Matt. 3:16, 17.*

27. How are the three divine Persons distinguished from each other?

The Father *has begotten* the Son from eternity; the Son *is begotten* of the Father from eternity; the Holy Ghost from eternity *proceeds* from the Father and the Son. — To the Father especially is ascribed the work of *Creation;* to the Son, the work of *Redemption;* to the Holy Ghost, the work of *Sanctification.*

51   Thou art My Son; this day *have I begotten Thee.* *Ps. 2:7.*

52   When the Comforter is come, whom *I will send* unto you from the Father, even the Spirit of Truth, which *proceedeth from the Father,* He shall testify of Me. *John 15:26.*

53   Because ye are sons, *God hath sent* forth the *Spirit of His Son* into your hearts, crying, Abba, Father. *Gal. 4:6.*

28. What does God forbid in the First Commandment?

God forbids *us to have other gods* instead of Him or beside Him. (Idolatry.)

54   Thou shalt worship the Lord, thy God, and *Him only* shalt thou serve. *Matt. 4:10.*

55   I am the Lord; that is My name; and *My glory will I not give to another,* neither My praise to graven images. *Is. 42:8.*

29. When do men have other gods?

Men have other gods —

A. When they regard and worship any creature as God;

NOTE. — See Is. 42:8. (Question 28.)

56   Our God is in the heavens; He hath done whatsoever He hath pleased. Their *idols are silver and gold,* the work of men's hands. *Ps. 115:3, 4.*

Bible Narratives: Israel worshiped the Golden Calf. *Ex. 32.* — The people worshiped Baal. *1 Kings 18:18-29.* — The Philistines made Dagon their god. *Judg. 16:23, 24.*

B. When they believe in a god who is not the Triune God;

57   All men should honor the Son even as they honor the Father. *He that honoreth not the Son honoreth not the Father*, which hath sent Him. *John 5:23.*

C. When they fear, love, or trust in any person or thing as they should fear, love, and trust in God alone.

58   *Fear not them which kill the body,* but are not able to kill the soul; but rather *fear Him* which is able to destroy both soul and body in hell. *Matt. 10:28.*

59   He that *loveth father or mother more than Me* is not worthy of Me; and he that loveth *son or daughter* more than Me is not worthy of Me. *Matt. 10:37.*

60   Trust in the Lord with all thine heart, and *lean not unto thine own understanding. Prov. 3:5.*

61   No whoremonger nor unclean person nor *covetous man,* who *is an idolater,* hath any inheritance in the kingdom of Christ and of God. *Eph. 5:5.*

62   How hard is it for them that *trust in riches* to enter into the kingdom of God! *Mark 10:24.*

63   Whose *god is their belly* and whose glory is in their shame, who mind earthly things. *Phil. 3:19.*

64   The *fool* hath said in his heart, *There is no God.* They are corrupt, they have done abominable works. *Ps. 14:1.* (Atheists.)

Bible Narratives: The rich man thought more of costly clothes and good eating than of God. *Luke 16:19.* — The rich young man loved his possessions more than Christ. *Matt. 19:22.*

30. What does God require of us in the First Commandment?

God requires that we *fear, love, and trust in Him* above all things.

31. When do we fear God above all things?

We fear God above all things when *with our whole heart we revere Him* as the highest Being, *honor Him with our lives,* and *avoid what displeases Him.*

65   Let all the earth *fear* the Lord; let all the inhabitants of the world *stand in awe* of Him. *Ps. 33:8.*

66   I am the almighty God; *walk before Me,* and be thou perfect. *Gen. 17:1.*

67   How, then, can I do this great wickedness and sin against God? *Gen. 39:9.*

68   The fear of the Lord is to hate evil. *Prov. 8:13.*

Bible Narrative: The three men in the fiery furnace feared God more than the king. *Dan. 3.*

32. When do we love God above all things?

We love God above all things when *with our whole heart we cling to Him* as to our God and gladly devote our lives to His service.

69   Thou shalt love the Lord, thy God, *with all thy heart* and with *all thy soul* and with *all thy mind. Matt. 22:37.*

70   Whom have I in heaven but Thee? And there is *none* upon earth *that I desire beside Thee.* My flesh and my heart faileth; but *God* is the Strength of my heart and *my Portion forever. Ps. 73:25, 26.*

Bible Narrative: Abraham loved God more than his son. *Gen. 22.*

33. When do we trust in God above all things?

We trust in God above all things when *with our whole heart we commit our lives to His keeping* and rely upon Him for help in every need.

71   It is better to *trust in the Lord* than to put confidence in man. *Ps. 118:8.*

72   *Trust* in the Lord *with all thine heart. Prov. 3:5.*

Bible Narrative: David trusted in the Lord when he fought against Goliath. *1 Sam. 17:37, 46, 47.*

THE SECOND COMMANDMENT

GOD'S NAME

Thou shalt not take the name of the Lord, thy God, in vain.

What does this mean? We should fear and love God that we may not curse, swear, use witchcraft, lie, or deceive by His name, but call upon it in every trouble, pray, praise, and give thanks.

---

34. Why do we say in this and in the following Commandments, "We should fear and love God"?

The fulfillment of all Commandments *must flow from the fear and love of God.*

35. What is God's name?

God's name is —

A. Every name by which God has made Himself known, such as God, Lord, Almighty, Jesus Christ, Holy Ghost.

Jehovah

[73] I am the *Lord;* that is *My name. Is. 42:8.*

[74] This is His name whereby He shall be called, *The Lord Our Righteousness. Jer. 23:6.*

[75] Thou shalt call His name *Jesus. Matt. 1:21.*

NOTE. — See Ex. 3:13, 14; Deut. 28:58; Is. 43:15; 44:6; 47:4; Jer. 32:18.

B. Every statement in which God tells us about Himself.

[76] In all places where I *record My name* I will come unto thee, and I will bless thee. *Ex. 20:24.*

36. What does God forbid in the Second Commandment?

In the Second Commandment God forbids us *to use His name in vain.*

[77] The Lord will not hold him guiltless that taketh His name in vain. *Ex. 20:7.*

37. What is using God's name in vain?

Using God's name in vain is —

A. Employing any name of God *uselessly or carelessly* ("My God," "Good Lord," "Jesus Christ," etc.).

B. Cursing, swearing, using witchcraft, lying, or deceiving by His name.

38. What is cursing by God's name?

Cursing by God's name is —

A. *Blaspheming God* by speaking evil of Him or mocking Him.

78   Whosoever *curseth his God* shall bear his *sin. Lev. 24:15.*

Bible Narratives: The Jews reviled Jesus when He was hanging on the cross. *Matt. 27:39-43.* — Rabshakeh blasphemed the God of Israel. *2 Kings 18:28-35; 19:21, 22.*

B. *Calling down the anger and punishment* of God upon any person or thing.

79   [With the tongue] bless we God, even the Father; and therewith *curse we men,* which are made after the similitude of God. Out of the same mouth proceedeth blessing and cursing. My brethren, these things *ought not so to be. James 3:9, 10.*

Bible Narratives: The Jews cursed themselves and their children. *Matt. 27:25.* — Goliath cursed David. *1 Sam. 17:43.* — Peter cursed. *Matt. 26:74.*

39. What is swearing by God's name?

Swearing by God's name is taking an oath in which we *call upon God to witness the truth* of what we say or promise, and to punish us if we lie or break our promise.

80   *I call God for a record* upon my soul. *2 Cor. 1:23.*

40. When are we permitted, and even required, to swear by God's name?

We are permitted, and even required, to swear by God's name —

A. When we are called upon by the government; for example, when the court demands that witnesses tell the truth, the whole truth, and nothing but the truth.

81   Let every soul be subject unto the higher powers. *Rom. 13:1.*

Bible Narrative: Jesus permitted Himself to be put under oath by the government. *Matt. 26:63, 64.*

B. When an oath is necessary for the glory of God or the welfare of our neighbor.

82   Thou shalt fear the Lord, thy God, and serve Him, and *shalt swear* by His name. *Deut. 6:13.*

83   Men verily swear by the greater; and an oath for confirmation is to them an *end of all strife. Heb. 6:16.*

Bible Narratives: Abraham put his servant under oath. *Gen. 24:3.* — Paul swore. *2 Cor. 1:23.*

41. Which swearing is sinful?

Swearing which is done *falsely, thoughtlessly,* or in *sinful, uncertain,* or *unimportant matters.*

84   Ye have heard that it hath been said by them of old time, Thou shalt not forswear thyself, but shalt perform unto the Lord thine oaths. But I say unto you, Swear not at all: neither by heaven, for it is God's throne; nor by the earth, for it is His footstool; neither by Jerusalem, for it is the city of the great King. Neither shalt thou swear by thy head, because thou canst not make one hair white or black. But *let your communication be, Yea, yea; Nay, nay;* for whatsoever is *more than these cometh of evil. Matt. 5:33-37.*

85   Ye shall not swear by My name *falsely. Lev. 19:12.* (Perjury.)

Bible Narratives: Peter swore falsely and thus committed perjury. *Matt. 26:72.* — Certain Jews swore to commit murder. *Acts 23:12.* — Herod swore in an unknown and unimportant matter. *Matt. 14:6-9.*

42. What is using witchcraft by God's name?

Using witchcraft by God's name is —

A. *Using* God's name in order to perform *supernatural* things with the help of the devil, such as conjuring, fortunetelling, and consulting the dead.

86   There shall not be found among you anyone that maketh his son or his daughter to pass through the fire or that useth divination or an observer of times, or an enchanter, or a witch, or a charmer, or a consulter with familiar spirits, or a wizard, or a necromancer. For all that do these things are *an abomination unto the Lord;* and because of these abominations the Lord, thy God, doth drive them out from before thee. *Deut. 18:10-12.*

Bible Narrative: The Egyptian sorcerers performed supernatural things with the help of the devil. *Ex. 7 and 8.*

B. *Seeking the aid* of people who practice these and similar satanic arts.

87   Regard not them that have familiar spirits, neither *seek after wizards*, to be defiled by them. I am the Lord, your God. *Lev. 19:31.*

Bible Narrative: King Saul sought the help of the witch of Endor. *1 Sam. 28.*

43. What is lying and deceiving by God's name?

Lying and deceiving by God's name is —

A. Teaching false doctrine and saying that it is God's Word or revelation. (False prophets.)

88   In vain they do worship Me, *teaching for doctrines the commandments of men. Matt. 15:9.*

89   Behold, I am against the prophets, saith the Lord, that use *their* tongues and say, *He* saith. *Jer. 23:31.*

90   What thing soever I command you, observe to do it; *thou shalt not add* thereto *nor diminish* from it. *Deut. 12:32.*

Bible Narrative: The lie of a false prophet caused a prophet of God to be deceived and killed. *1 Kings 13:11-19.*

B. Covering up an unbelieving heart or a sinful life by a show of piety. (Hypocrites.)

91   This people draweth nigh unto Me with their *mouth* and honoreth Me with their *lips;* but their *heart is far from Me. Matt. 15:8.*

92   Not everyone that *saith unto Me, Lord, Lord,* shall enter into the kingdom of heaven; but he that *doeth* the will of My Father which is in heaven. *Matt. 7:21.*

Bible Narratives: The scribes and the Pharisees were hypocrites. *Matt. 23:13-33.* — Ananias and Sapphira were hypocrites. *Acts 5:1-11.*

44. What does God require of us in the Second Commandment?

We should *call upon His name* in every trouble, *pray, praise, and give thanks.*

93   *Call upon Me* in the day of trouble. I will deliver thee, and *thou shalt glorify Me. Ps. 50:15.*

94   *Ask,* and it shall be given you; *seek,* and ye shall find; *knock,* and it shall be opened unto you. *Matt. 7:7.*

95   *Bless the Lord,* O my soul, and all that is within me, *bless His holy name. Ps. 103:1.*

96   *Oh, give thanks* unto the Lord, for He is good; because His mercy endureth forever. *Ps. 118:1.*

Bible Narratives: The ten lepers called upon Jesus in their trouble. *Luke 17:11-13.* — The grateful stranger thanked Jesus and glorified God for the healing. *Luke 17:15, 16.* — Hannah petitioned and thanked God for the gift of a son. *1 Sam. 1 and 2.*

Thy Word Is
a Lamp

THE THIRD COMMANDMENT

GOD'S WORD

Remember the Sabbath day, to keep it holy. (Thou shalt sanctify the holy day.)

What does this mean? We should fear and love God that we may not despise preaching and His Word, but hold it sacred and gladly hear and learn it.

45. Does God require that we Christians of the New Testament observe the Sabbath (Saturday) and other holy days of the Old Testament?

He does not; for in the New Testament the Sabbath and other holy days were *abolished by God Himself.*

97   The Son of Man is *Lord even of the Sabbath day.* Matt. 12:8.

98   Let no man therefore judge you in meat or in drink or in *respect of an holy day* or of the new moon or of the *Sabbath days;* which are a *shadow of things to come;* but the *body is of Christ. Col. 2:16, 17.*

46. Did God command us Christians to observe any day?

God did *not* command us Christians to observe *any day*.

99　One man esteemeth one day above another; another esteemeth every day alike. Let every man be fully persuaded in his own mind. He that regardeth the day regardeth it unto the Lord; and he that regardeth not the day, to the Lord he doth not regard it. *Rom. 14:5, 6*.

100　Ye observe days and months and times and years. I am afraid of you lest I have bestowed upon you labor in vain. *Gal. 4:10, 11*.

47. Why, then, do we observe Sunday and other church festivals?

We observe Sunday and other church festivals in order *to have time and opportunity for public worship*.

101　*Not forsaking the assembling* of ourselves together, as the manner of some is. *Heb. 10:25*.

102　They *continued steadfastly* in the Apostles' doctrine and fellowship and in breaking of bread and in prayers. *Acts 2:42*.

Bible Narrative: The early Christians observed the first day of the week. *Acts 20:7; 1 Cor. 16:2*.

48. How does our Catechism explain the Third Commandment in the New Testament sense?

We should fear and love God that we may *not despise preaching and His Word*, but *hold it sacred* and *gladly hear and learn it*.

49. When do we sin against the Third Commandment?

We sin against the Third Commandment when we *despise preaching and the Word of God.*

50. How is this done?

We despise preaching and the Word of God —

A. When we do *not attend public worship;*

B. When we do *not use the written Word of God and the Sacraments;*

C. When we use the Word of God and the Sacraments *negligently* or *carelessly.*

103   He that is of God heareth God's words; ye therefore *hear them not* because ye *are not of God. John 8:47.*

104   He that heareth you heareth Me; and he that *despiseth you despiseth Me;* and he that despiseth Me despiseth Him that sent Me. *Luke 10:16.*

Bible Narratives: The scribes and the Pharisees despised Baptism. *Luke 7:30.* — Saul rejected the Word of God. *1 Sam. 15:10-23.*

NOTE. — See Acts 13:45, 46.

51. What does God require of us in the Third Commandment?

A. We should *hold preaching and the Word of God sacred.*

105   When ye received the Word of God which ye heard of us, ye received it not as the word of men, but, *as it is in truth, the Word of God. 1 Thess. 2:13.*

106   To this man will I look, even to him that is poor and of a contrite spirit and *trembleth at My Word. Is. 66:2.*

B. We should gladly *hear it, learn it,* and *meditate upon it.*

107   Keep thy foot when thou goest to the house of God, and be more ready to *hear* than to give the sacrifice of fools; for they consider not that they do evil. *Eccl. 5:1.*

108   Lord, I have *loved the habitation of Thy house* and the place where Thine honor dwelleth. *Ps. 26:8.*

109   They *continued steadfastly* in the Apostles' doctrine and fellowship and in breaking of bread and in prayers. *Acts 2:42.*

110   Let the Word of Christ *dwell in you richly. Col. 3:16.*

111   This Book of the Law shall not depart out of thy mouth; but thou shalt *meditate therein* day and night. *Josh. 1:8.*

112   Blessed are they that hear the Word of God and *keep* it. *Luke 11:28.*

Bible Narratives: Jesus gladly heard and learned the Word of God. *Luke 2:41-52.* — Mary sat at the feet of Jesus and learned His Word. *Luke 10:39.* — Mary kept and pondered the Word of God in her heart. *Luke 2:19.* — The Bereans searched the Scriptures daily. *Acts 17:11.*

C. We should honor and support the preaching and teaching of the Word of God.

113   *Obey them* that have the rule over you, and *submit yourselves;* for they watch for your souls as they that must give account, that they may do it with joy and not with grief; for that is unprofitable for you. *Heb. 13:17.*

114   Let him that is taught in the Word *communicate unto him that teacheth* in all good things. Be not deceived; God is not mocked; for whatsoever a man soweth, that shall he also reap. *Gal. 6:6, 7.*

NOTE. — See 1 Cor. 9:11.

Bible Narrative: The poor widow gave money for the upkeep of the Temple and for the support of the priests. *Mark 12: 41-44.*

NOTE. — See also "What the Hearers Owe to Their Pastors" under the Table of Duties, page 25.

D. We should diligently spread the Word of God.

115   *Go ye into all the world and preach* the Gospel to every creature. *Mark 16:15.* (Missions.)

THE SECOND TABLE

52. What is the summary of the Second Table of the Law?

"Thou shalt lóve thy *neighbor* as thyself." *Matt. 22:39.*

53. Who is our neighbor?

Our neighbor is every one of our *fellow men.*

116   As we have therefore opportunity, let us do good unto *all men*, especially unto them who are of the *household of faith. Gal. 6:10.*

117   Lové your *enemies. Matt. 5:44.*

Bible Narrative: The good Samaritan had compassion on his enemy and showed him mercy. *Luke 10:25-37.*

54. How should we love our neighbor?

We should love our neighbor *as ourselves* and show this love by keeping the Commandments of the Second Table.

118   All things whatsoever ye would that men should do to you, do ye even so to them; for this is the Law and the Prophets. *Matt. 7:12.*

THE FOURTH COMMANDMENT

THE AUTHORITIES WHOM GOD HAS PLACED OVER US

Thou shalt honor thy father and thy mother, that it may be well with thee, and thou mayest live long on the earth.

What does this mean? We should fear and love God that we may not despise our parents and masters, nor provoke them to anger, but give them honor, serve and obey them, and hold them in love and esteem.

---

55. Who are parents and masters?

Parents are *father and mother;* masters are all those who by God's ordinance are placed over us in the *home,* in the *state,* at *school,* and at the *place where we work.*

56. What does God forbid in the Fourth Commandment?

God forbids us to *despise* our parents and other superiors by *disregarding their dignity* or *provoking* them to just anger by *disobedience* or by any other kind of *wickedness.*

119   The eye that *mocketh* at his father and *despiseth* to obey his mother, the ravens of the valley shall pick it out, and the young eagles shall eat it. *Prov.* 30:17.

120 Whosoever therefore resisteth the power *resisteth the ordinance of God;* and they that resist shall receive to themselves damnation. *Rom. 13:2.* (Government.)

NOTE.—See "To Servants, Hired Men, and Employees" under the Table of Duties, page 29.

Bible Narratives: The sons of Eli grieved their father by their wickedness. *1 Sam. 2:12, 23, 25.* — Absalom rebelled against his father and king. *2 Sam. 15.*

57. What does God require of us in the Fourth Commandment?

God requires us —

A. To *honor* our parents and other superiors, that is, to *regard them as God's representatives;*

121 *Honor thy father and mother;* which is the first commandment with promise: that it may be well with thee and thou mayest live long on the earth. *Eph. 6:2, 3.*

122 Thou shalt rise up before the *hoary head* and honor the face of the *old man. Lev. 19:32.*

NOTE. — See "To Parents" and "To Children" under the Table of Duties, page 28.

Bible Narratives: Joseph honored his father. *Gen. 46:29.* — King Solomon honored his mother. *1 Kings 2:19.* — Elisha honored his teacher. *2 Kings 2:12.*

B. To *serve* our parents and other superiors by gladly *doing for them what we can;*

123 Let them learn first to show piety at home and to *requite their parents;* for that is good and acceptable before God. *1 Tim. 5:4.*

Bible Narratives: Joseph provided for his father. *Gen. 47: 11, 12.* — Jesus provided for His mother. *John 19:26.*

c. To *obey* our parents and other superiors in all things in which God has placed them over us;

124   Children, *obey your parents* in all things; for this is well pleasing unto the Lord. *Col. 3:20.*

125   *Hearken* unto thy father that begat thee, and despise not thy mother when she is old. *Prov. 23:22.*

126   Servants, be *subject to your masters* with all fear; not only to the good and gentle, but also to the froward. *1 Peter 2:18.*

127   We ought to obey *God rather than men. Acts 5:29.*

NOTE. — See "To Servants, Hired Men, and Employees," "To Employers," page 29, and "Of Subjects," page 27.

Bible Narratives: Jesus was subject to Mary and Joseph. *Luke 2:51.* — Jonathan disobeyed his father in order to spare David's life and thus obeyed God rather than man. *1 Sam. 20:31-33.*

D. To *love* and *esteem* our parents and superiors as *precious gifts of God.*

58. Why does God add the promise "that it may be well with thee and thou mayest live long on the earth"?

By this promise God *impresses upon us the importance and benefit* of honoring our parents and superiors and urges us to obey this Commandment willingly.

THE FIFTH COMMANDMENT

HUMAN LIFE AND WELL-BEING

Thou shalt not kill.

What does this mean? We should fear and love God that we may not hurt nor harm our neighbor in his body, but help and befriend him in every bodily need.

---

59. What does God forbid in the Fifth Commandment?

A. God forbids us to *take the life of a fellow man* (murder) or *our own life* (suicide).

128 Whoso *sheddeth man's blood,* by man shall his blood be shed; for in the image of God made He man. *Gen. 9:6.*

129 All they that *take the sword* shall perish with the sword. *Matt. 26:52.* (Capital punishment.)

130 He [the government] beareth not the sword in vain; for he is the *minister of God, a revenger to execute wrath* upon him that doeth evil. *Rom. 13:4.* (The government has the right to inflict the death penalty and to wage just wars.)

Bible Narratives: Cain killed his brother Abel. *Gen. 4:8.* — David killed Uriah through others. *2 Sam. 11:15.* — Killing through carelessness. *Ex. 21:29; Deut. 22:8.* — Judas killed himself. *Matt. 27:5.*

B. God forbids us to hurt or harm our neighbor in his body, that is, to *do or say anything* which may *destroy, shorten, or embitter* his life.

131   Dearly beloved, *avenge not yourselves*, but rather give place unto wrath; for it is written, Vengeance is Mine; I will repay, saith the Lord. *Rom. 12:19*.

Bible Narratives: Joseph's brothers harmed Joseph and embittered the life of their father by their wickedness. *Gen. 37: 23-35.* — The Egyptians embittered the lives of the children of Israel by hard labor. *Ex. 1.*

c. God forbids us to *bear anger and hatred* in our hearts against our neighbor.

132   I say unto you, That whosoever is *angry with his brother* without a cause shall be in danger of the judgment. *Matt. 5:22*.

133   Whosoever *hateth his brother is a murderer;* and ye know that no murderer hath eternal life abiding in him. *1 John 3:15*.

134   Out of the heart proceed *evil thoughts, murders*, adulteries, fornications, thefts, false witness, blasphemies. *Matt. 15:19*.

135   Be ye angry, and sin not; let not the sun go down upon your wrath. *Eph. 4:26*.

Bible Narratives: The Jews showed their anger against Stephen. *Acts 7:54.* — God warned Cain against anger. *Gen. 4:5-7.*

60. What does God require of us in the Fifth Commandment?

a. We should *help and befriend* our neighbor in every bodily need.

136   If thine enemy hunger, *feed him;* if he thirst, *give him drink;* for in so doing, thou shalt heap coals of fire on his head. *Rom. 12:20*.

Bible Narratives: Abraham rescued Lot from his enemies. *Gen. 14:12-16.* — David protected the life of Saul. *1 Sam. 26:1-12.* — The good Samaritan helped the man who had fallen among thieves. *Luke 10:33-35.*

B. We should be *merciful, kind,* and *forgiving* towards our neighbor.

137   Blessed are the meek; for they shall inherit the earth. Blessed are the *merciful;* for they shall obtain mercy. Blessed are the *peacemakers;* for they shall be called the children of God. *Matt. 5:5, 7, 9.*

138   *Agree with thine adversary quickly,* while thou art in the way with him, lest at any time the adversary deliver thee to the judge, and the judge deliver thee to the officer, and thou be cast into prison. *Matt. 5:25.*

139   If ye *forgive* not men their trespasses, neither will your Father forgive your trespasses. *Matt. 6:15.*

140   Be ye *kind* one to another, *tenderhearted, forgiving* one another, even as God for Christ's sake hath forgiven you. *Eph. 4:32.*

Bible Narratives: Jesus showed mercy to the ten lepers. *Luke 17:11-19.* — The centurion was kind to his sick servant. *Matt. 8:5-13.* — Joseph was forgiving toward his brothers. *Gen. 45:1-16.*

THE SIXTH COMMANDMENT

MARRIAGE AND PURITY

Thou shalt not commit adultery.

What does this mean? We should fear and love God that we may lead a chaste and decent life in word and deed, and each love and honor his spouse.

61. What is marriage?

Marriage is the *lifelong union of one man and one woman unto one flesh.* Marriage was *instituted by God* and is entered into by *rightful betrothal,* or engagement.

Holy Wedlock

141   They are no more twain, but *one flesh. What therefore God hath joined together let not man put asunder.* Matt. 19:6.

Bible Narratives: The institution of marriage. *Gen. 2:18-24.* — The angel calls Mary, who was engaged to Joseph, Joseph's wife and calls Joseph her husband. *Matt. 1:19, 20, 24.*

62. What does God forbid in the Sixth Commandment?

A. God forbids the *breaking of the marriage vow* by unfaithfulness or desertion. He permits the innocent party to procure a divorce when the other party is guilty of fornication.

142   What therefore God hath joined together let *not man put asunder.* Matt. 19:6.

143   Whosoever shall *put away his wife, except it be for fornication,* and shall marry another, committeth adultery. Matt. 19:9.

144   Whoremongers and adulterers God will judge. Heb. 13:4.

Bible Narratives: David committed adultery with the wife of Uriah. *2 Sam. 11.* — Herod took his brother's wife. *Mark 6:18.*

B. God also forbids all *unchaste and unclean thoughts, desires, words, and deeds.*

[145]   Out of the heart proceed *evil thoughts*, murders, *adulteries*, *fornications*, thefts, false witness, blasphemies *Matt. 15:19*.

[146]   Whosoever looketh on a woman *to lust after her* hath committed adultery with her already *in his heart*. *Matt. 5:28*.

[147]   *Fornication* and *all uncleanness* or covetousness, let it not be once named among you, as becometh saints; neither *filthiness* nor *foolish talking* nor *jesting*, which are not convenient, but rather giving of thanks. *Eph. 5:3, 4*.

[148]   It is a shame even to *speak* of those things which are done of them *in secret*. *Eph. 5:12*.

Bible Narratives: Potiphar's wife, with lust in her heart, cast her eyes upon Joseph. *Gen. 39:7-12*. — Samson committed fornication. *Judg. 16:1*.

63. What does God require of all of us in the Sixth Commandment?

We should lead a *chaste and decent* life in thoughts, desires, words, and deeds.

[149]   *Abstain from fleshly lusts,* which war against the soul. *1 Peter 2:11*.

[150]   Whatsoever things are pure . . . whatsoever things are of *good report;* if there be any *virtue,* and if there be any praise, think on these things. *Phil. 4:8*.

[151]   Let no corrupt communication proceed out of your mouth, but that which is *good to the use of edifying,* that it may minister grace unto the hearers. *Eph. 4:29*.

64. What must we do to lead a chaste and decent life?

In the fear of God we must —

A. *Fight to overcome* all impure thoughts and desires with God's Word and prayer, work and temperance;

¹⁵²   How, then, can I do this great wickedness and sin against God? *Gen. 39:9.*

¹⁵³   Create in me a *clean heart,* O God. *Ps. 51:10.*

¹⁵⁴   *Look not thou upon the wine* when it is red, when it giveth his color in the cup, when it moveth itself aright. At the last it biteth like a serpent and stingeth like an adder. Thine eyes *shall behold strange women,* and thine *heart shall utter perverse things. Prov. 23:31-33.*

B. *Flee and avoid* every opportunity for un-chasteness.

¹⁵⁵   Flee fornication. *1 Cor. 6:18.*

¹⁵⁶   Flee also youthful lusts. *2 Tim. 2:22.*

¹⁵⁷   Know ye not that your body is the *temple of the Holy Ghost,* which is in you, which ye have of God, and ye are *not your own? 1 Cor. 6:19.*

¹⁵⁸   My son, if *sinners entice* thee, *consent thou not. Prov. 1:10.*

Bible Narrative: Joseph resisted the temptation of Potiphar's wife and fled from her. *Gen. 39:7-12.*

65. What does God require of married people especially?

God requires married people to *love and honor each other,* the husband his wife as *his God-given helpmeet* and the wife her husband as *her God-given head.*

¹⁵⁹   As the Church is subject unto Christ, so let the *wives* be to *their own husbands* in everything. *Husbands, love your wives,* even as Christ also loved the Church and gave Himself for it. *Eph. 5:24, 25.*

NOTE. — See "To Husbands" and "To Wives" under the Table of Duties, page 28.

THE SEVENTH COMMANDMENT

PROPERTY AND BUSINESS

Thou shalt not steal.

What does this mean? We should fear and love God that we may not take our neighbor's money or goods, nor get them by false ware or dealing, but help him to improve and protect his property and business.

66. What particular sins does God forbid in the Seventh Commandment?

God forbids every kind of *robbery, theft,* and *fraud,* as well as *sinful longing* for anything that belongs to our neighbor.

160   Let him that stole, steal no more; but rather let him labor, working with his hands the thing which is good, that he may have to give to him that needeth. *Eph. 4:28.*

161   Ye shall do *no unrighteousness* in judgment, in mete-yard, in weight, or in measure. *Lev. 19:35.*

162   Woe unto him that buildeth his house *by unrighteous-ness* and his chambers *by wrong;* that *useth his neighbor's service without wages* and giveth him not for his work! *Jer. 22:13.*

163   If any *would not work,* neither should he eat. *2 Thess. 3:10.*

164   The wicked borroweth and payeth not again. *Ps. 37:21.*

165 Whoso is *partner with a thief* hateth his own soul. *Prov. 29:24.*

166 Out of the heart proceed *evil thoughts*, murders, adulteries, fornications, *thefts*, false witness, blasphemies. *Matt. 15:19.*

Bible Narratives: The men who fell upon the traveler on the way to Jericho robbed him. *Luke 10:30.* — Achan stole when he secretly took a garment and silver and gold. *Josh. 7:20-22.* — Judas was a thief. *John 12:6.* — Gehazi obtained a present by lying and trickery. *2 Kings 5:20-24.*

67. What does God require of us in the Seventh Commandment?

A. We should *help our neighbor to improve and protect his property and business*.

167 If thou meet thine enemy's ox or his ass going astray, thou shalt surely *bring it back to him again. Ex. 23:4.*

168 Whatsoever ye would that men should do to you, *do ye even so to them. Matt. 7:12.*

Bible Narratives: Abraham gave Lot the choice of the land. *Gen. 13:9.* — Abraham rescued Lot from the enemy and recovered his property. *Gen. 14:12-16.*

B. We should *help him in every need*.

169 *Give to him* that asketh thee, and from him that would borrow of thee *turn not thou away. Matt. 5:42.*

170 He that hath *pity upon the poor* lendeth unto the Lord; and that which he hath given will He pay him again. *Prov. 19:17.*

171 To *do good* and to *communicate* forget not; for with such sacrifices God is well pleased. *Heb. 13:16.*

Bible Narrative: Zacchaeus promised to restore fourfold what he had taken by fraud and to give half of his goods to the poor. *Luke 19:8.*

C. We should *rejoice when we see him prosper*.

172 Charity *envieth not . . . seeketh not* her own. *1 Cor. 13:4, 5.*

THE EIGHTH COMMANDMENT

GOOD REPUTATION

Thou shalt not bear false witness against thy neighbor.

What does this mean? We should fear and love God that we may not deceitfully belie, betray, slander, nor defame our neighbor, but defend him, speak well of him, and put the best construction on everything.

---

68. What does God forbid in the Eighth Commandment?

A. God forbids us to *make any untrue statement* against our neighbor *in court*.

173 *A false witness* shall not be unpunished. *Prov. 19:5.*

Bible Narratives: False witnesses arose against Jesus. *Matt. 26:59-61.* — False witnesses arose against Naboth. *1 Kings 21:13.*

B. God forbids us to *belie* our neighbor; that is, to *lie about him or lie to him* or *withhold from him the truth* in order to harm him.

174 He that *speaketh lies* shall not escape. *Prov. 19:5.*

175 *Putting away lying,* speak every man truth with his neighbor; for we are members one of another. *Eph. 4:25.*

Bible Narrative: Gehazi lied about Elisha and then lied to him. *2 Kings 5:22, 25.*

C. God forbids us to *betray* our neighbor; that is, to *reveal his secrets.*

176 A talebearer *revealeth secrets;* but he that is of a faithful spirit concealeth the matter. *Prov. 11:13.*

Bible Narratives: Doeg betrayed Ahimelech. *1 Sam. 22: 6-19.* — Judas betrayed Jesus. *Matt. 26:14-16.*

D. God forbids us to *slander or defame* our neighbor; that is, to *speak evil* of him and thus *injure or destroy his good name.*

177 *Speak not evil* one of another, brethren. *James 4:11.*

178 [Unto the wicked God saith:] Thou givest thy mouth to evil, and thy tongue frameth deceit. Thou sittest and *speakest against* thy brother; thou *slanderest* thine own mother's son. These things hast thou done, and I kept silence; thou thoughtest that I was altogether such an one as thyself. But I will reprove thee and set them in order before thine eyes. Now consider this, ye that forget God, lest I *tear you in pieces* and there be none to deliver. *Ps. 50:19-22.*

179 *Judge not,* and ye shall not be judged; *condemn not,* and ye shall not be condemned. *Luke 6:37.*

180 If thy brother shall trespass against thee, go and tell him his fault *between thee and him alone. Matt. 18:15.*

Bible Narrative: Absalom slandered his father. *2 Sam. 15:1-6.*

E. God forbids us to have *evil thoughts* against our neighbor or to plot against him.

181 Let none of you *imagine evil* in your hearts against his neighbor. *Zech. 8:17.*

69. What does God require of us in the Eighth Commandment?

A. We should *defend* our neighbor; that is, we should *take his part and shield him* against false accusations.

182   *Open thy mouth for the dumb* in the cause of all such as are appointed to destruction. Open thy mouth, judge righteously, and *plead the cause* of the poor and needy. *Prov. 31:8, 9.*

B. We should *speak well* of our neighbor; that is, we should *praise his good qualities and deeds* so far as it can be done in keeping with the truth.

Bible Narratives: Jonathan spoke well of David. *1 Sam. 19:4.* — The people of Capernaum spoke well of the centurion. *Luke 7:4, 5.*

C. We should put the *best construction* on everything; that is, we should *cover up his faults and explain in his favor* whatever can be so explained.

183   Charity shall *cover the multitude of sins. 1 Peter 4:8.*

184   Charity believeth all things, hopeth all things, endureth all things. *1 Cor. 13:7.*

THE NINTH COMMANDMENT

A HOLY HEART

Thou shalt not covet thy neighbor's house.

What does this mean? We should fear and love God that we may not craftily seek to get our neighbor's inheritance or house, nor obtain it by a show of right, but help and be of service to him in keeping it.

70. What does God forbid in the Ninth Commandment?

God forbids coveting, that is, having a sinful *desire* for anything that belongs to our neighbor.

71. What will such sinful desire move us to do?

Such sinful desire will move us *to seek to get* our neighbor's inheritance or house *by trickery or by a show of right.*

185   Woe unto them that *join house to house,* that *lay field to field,* till there be no place, that they may be placed alone in the midst of the earth! *Is. 5:8.*

186   Woe unto you, scribes and Pharisees, hypocrites! For ye *devour widows' houses* and for a *pretense make long prayer;* therefore ye shall receive the greater damnation. *Matt. 23:14.*

187   Having food and raiment, let us be therewith content. But they that *will be rich* fall into temptation and a snare and into many foolish and hurtful lusts, which drown men in destruction and perdition. For the *love of money* is the *root of all evil,* which while some *coveted after,* they have *erred from the faith* and pierced themselves through with many sorrows. *1 Tim. 6:8-10.*

Bible Narrative: Ahab coveted Naboth's vineyard and obtained it by a show of right. *1 Kings 21:1-16.*

72. What does God require of us in the Ninth Commandment?

God requires that our hearts be filled with *holy desires only*.

188   Ye shall *be holy;* for I, the Lord, your God, am holy. *Lev. 19:2.*

73. What will such holy desires move us to do?

Such holy desires will move us to *help* our neighbor and *be of service* to him in keeping his inheritance or house.

189   By love serve one another. *Gal. 5:13.*

THE TENTH COMMANDMENT

A HOLY HEART

Thou shalt not covet thy neighbor's wife, nor his manservant, nor his maidservant, nor his cattle, nor anything that is thy neighbor's.

What does this mean? We should fear and love God that we may not estrange, force, or entice away from our neighbor his wife, servants, or cattle, but urge them to stay and do their duty.

---

74. What does God forbid also in the Tenth Commandment?

God forbids, also in the Tenth Commandment, the sin of covetousness.

75. What will such covetousness move us to do?

Such covetousness will move us to *try to get* our neighbor's wife, servants, or cattle *away from him.*

Bible Narratives: David coveted Uriah's wife and took her. *2 Sam. 11:2-4.* — Absalom estranged the hearts of the people from David. *2 Sam. 15:1-6.*

76. What does God require of us in the Tenth Commandment?

God requires that our hearts be filled with *holy desires only.*

77. What will such holy desires move us to do?

Such holy desires will move us to *urge our neighbor's wife and servants to stay* with him and do their duty.

Bible Narrative: Paul returned a runaway servant to his master Philemon. *Epistle to Philemon.*

78. What does God particularly impress upon us in the last two Commandments?

God impresses upon us —

A. That in His sight *evil desire,* or *lust,* is indeed *sin and deserves condemnation;*

190   I had not known lust except the Law had said, *Thou shalt not covet. Rom. 7:7.*

191   Every man is tempted when he is drawn away of his own *lust* and enticed. Then, when *lust* hath conceived, it *bringeth forth sin;* and *sin,* when it is finished, *bringeth forth death. James 1:14, 15.*

B. That we should not have *any evil lust whatever* in our hearts, but only *holy desires* and *love of God and of all that is good.*

192   *Ye shall be holy;* for I, the Lord, your God, am holy. *Lev. 19:2.*

193   Be ye therefore *perfect,* even as your Father which is in heaven is perfect. *Matt. 5:48.*

194   *Delight thyself also in the Lord;* and He shall give thee the desires of thine heart. *Ps. 37:4.*

THE CLOSE OF THE COMMANDMENTS
THREAT AND PROMISE

What does God say of all these Commandments? He says thus:

I, the Lord, thy God, am a jealous God, visiting the iniquity of the fathers upon the children unto the third and fourth generation of them that hate Me, and showing mercy unto thousands of them that love Me and keep My Commandments.

What does this mean? God threatens to punish all that transgress these Commandments. Therefore we should fear His wrath and not act contrary to them. But He promises grace and every blessing to all that keep these Commandments. Therefore we should also love and trust in Him and willingly do according to His Commandments.

79. Why does God say, "I, the Lord, thy God, am a jealous God"?

By these words God teaches us —

A. That He has *a right to give us these* Commandments ("Lord, thy God");

B. That He *insists on strict and perfect* obedience ("jealous").

80. With what does God threaten all that hate Him and transgress His Commandments?

God threatens them with His *wrath and displeasure, temporal death and eternal damnation.*

195   *Cursed* is everyone that continueth not in all things which are written in the Book of the Law to do them. *Gal. 3:10.*

196   The wages of sin is death. *Rom. 6:23.*

81. Whom does God threaten to punish?

God threatens to punish *all* that transgress His Commandments.

197   The soul *that sinneth*, it shall die. The son shall not bear the iniquity of the father, neither shall the father bear the iniquity of the son; the righteousness of the righteous shall be upon him, and *the wickedness of the wicked shall be upon him. Ezek. 18:20.*

82. What does God mean when He threatens to visit the iniquity of the fathers upon the children unto the third and fourth generation of them that hate Him?

If the children, grandchildren, and great-grandchildren also hate God and follow in the

evil ways of their parents, then God will during
their earthly lives punish them for the sins of
their ancestors.

Bible Narratives: The wicked descendants of Ham bear the
curse of their ancestor's sin. *Gen. 9:25.* — The wicked Jews
bear the curse of their ancestors' sin. *Matt. 27:25.*

83. Why does God threaten such punishment?

God threatens such punishment to make us
fear His wrath, so that we do not act contrary to
His Commandments.

Bible Narratives: The Deluge destroyed the wicked world.
Gen. 7. — Wicked Sodom was destroyed. *Gen. 19.* — The
wickedness of the Jews brought about the destruction of
Jerusalem. *Luke 19:43, 44.*

84. What does God mean by promising grace and every blessing to those who love Him and keep His Commandments?

God will *graciously reward* in body and soul
all those who love Him and keep His Commandments.

198   Godliness is profitable unto all things, having promise
of the *life that now is* and of that which *is to come.*
1 Tim. 4:8.

199   I am *not worthy* of the least of all the mercies and of
all the truth which Thou hast showed unto Thy servant.
Gen. 32:10.

85. What does God mean by promising mercy unto thousands of them that love Him and keep His Commandments?

God will bless the descendants of His loving
and obedient children *for many generations.*

Bible Narratives: God blessed the Israelites for the sake of
pious Abraham. He also blessed the kings of Judah for the
sake of David.

86. Why does God add such promises?

God would by these promises move us *to
love Him, to trust in Him,* and *willingly to do*
according to His Commandments.

200   This is the love of God, that we keep His Commandments. *1 John 5:3.*

THE FULFILLMENT OF THE LAW

87. How does God want us to keep His Com-
mandments?

God wants us to keep His Commandments
perfectly in *thoughts, desires, words,* and *deeds.*

201   Be ye therefore *perfect,* even as your Father which is
in heaven is perfect. *Matt. 5:48.*

202   Whosoever shall keep the whole Law and yet *offend
in one point,* he is *guilty of all. James 2:10.*

88. Can man keep God's Commandments as He
wants us to keep them?

A. Since the fall into sin natural man cannot
keep the Law of God.

203   They are all gone aside, they are all together become
filthy; there is *none that doeth good, no, not one. Ps. 14:3.*

204   There is *not a just man upon earth* that doeth good
and sinneth not. *Eccl. 7:20.*

205   We are *all* as an *unclean* thing, and all our righteous-
nesses are as *filthy* rags. *Is. 64:6.*

B. Even Christians can keep it only imperfectly.

206   *Not* as though I had already attained, either were already *perfect;* but I follow after, if that I may apprehend that for which also I am apprehended of Christ Jesus. *Phil. 3:12.*

207   Enter not into judgment with Thy *servant;* for in Thy sight shall *no man living be justified. Ps. 143:2.*

208   If we say that we have no sin, we deceive ourselves, and the truth is not in us. *1 John 1:8.*

89. Can anyone, then, be saved by the Law?

"No man is justified by the Law in the sight of God." *Gal. 3:11.*

THE PURPOSE OF THE LAW

90. What, then, is the purpose of the Law?

The Law has a threefold purpose:

First, the Law checks to some extent the coarse outbursts of sin and thereby helps to *keep order* in the world. *(A curb.)*

209   The Law is not made for a righteous man, but *for the lawless and disobedient,* for the *ungodly* and for *sinners,* for *unholy* and *profane,* for *murderers* of fathers and *murderers* of mothers. *1 Tim. 1:9.*

210   When the Gentiles, which have not the Law, do by nature the things contained in the Law, these, having not the Law, are a law unto themselves; which show the work of the Law written in their hearts, their conscience also bearing witness, and their thoughts the meanwhile accusing or else excusing one another. *Rom. 2:14, 15.*

Secondly, the Law *shows us our sins.* *(A mirror.)*

211   By the Law is the *knowledge of sin. Rom. 3:20.*

212   I had not known sin but by the Law; for I had not known *lust* except the Law had said, *Thou shalt not covet. Rom.* 7:7.

Thirdly, the Law teaches us Christians which works we must do to *lead a God-pleasing life. (A rule.)*

213   Wherewithal shall a young man cleanse his way? By *taking heed thereto according to Thy Word. Ps. 119:9.*

214   Thy Word is a *lamp unto my feet* and a *light unto my path. Ps. 119:105.*

NOTE. — See Luke 10:27.

SIN

91. What is sin?

"Sin is the transgression of the Law." *1 John 3:4.*

NOTE. — Other names for sin are: disobedience, Rom. 5:19; debts, Matt. 6:12; transgression, iniquity, Ex. 34:7; fault, Matt. 18:15; trespass, 2 Cor. 5:19; unrighteousness, Rom. 6:13; wrong, Col. 3:25.

Sin Encircling
the World

92. By whom was sin brought into the world?

Sin was brought into the world by the *devil*, who was once a holy angel but fell away from God, and by *man*, who of his own free will yielded to the temptation of the devil.

215   He that committeth sin is of the devil; for *the devil sinneth from the beginning. 1 John 3:8.*

216   *By one man* sin entered into the world. *Rom. 5:12.*

Bible Narrative: The fall of man. *Gen. 3:1-7.*

93. How many kinds of sin are there?

There are *two kinds* of sin: *original* sin and *actual* sin.

94. What is original sin?

Original sin (inherited sin) is the *total corruption* of our *whole human nature.*

217   Behold, I was shapen in iniquity, and in sin did my mother conceive me. *Ps. 51:5.*

218   That which is *born of the flesh is flesh;* and that which is born of the Spirit is spirit. *John 3:6.*

219   Put off concerning the former conversation the *old man,* which *is corrupt* according to the deceitful lusts. *Eph. 4:22.*

95. How may this inherited corruption be more fully described?

Man by nature is without true fear, love, and trust in God. He is without righteousness, is inclined only to evil, and is spiritually blind, dead, and an enemy of God.

220   The imagination of man's heart is *evil from his youth. Gen. 8:21.*

NOTE. — See also Gen. 6:5; Eph. 4:18; Rom. 3:11, 12.

221   I know that in me (that is, in my flesh) dwelleth *no good thing. Rom. 7:18.*

222 The natural man *receiveth not* the things of the Spirit of God, for they are foolishness unto him; neither can he know them, because they are spiritually discerned. *1 Cor. 2:14.*

223 [Ye] were *dead* in trespasses and sins. *Eph. 2:1.*

224 The carnal mind is *enmity* against God. *Rom. 8:7.*

Bible Narrative: Seth was born in the image of his sinful father. *Gen. 5:3.*

96. In what condition is man by nature on account of original sin?

On account of original sin, man is by nature *lost and condemned, ruined in body and soul.*

225 [We] were by nature the *children of wrath,* even as others. *Eph. 2:3.*

226 *Death* passed upon all men, for that all have sinned. *Rom. 5:12.*

227 The wages of sin is *death. Rom. 6:23.*

97. How does original sin show itself in our lives?

Original sin causes us to *commit* all manner of *actual* sins.

228 A *corrupt tree* bringeth forth *evil fruit. Matt. 7:17.*

98. What is actual sin?

Actual sin is *every act* against a commandment of God in thoughts, desires, words, or deeds.

229 Out of the heart proceed *evil thoughts,* murders, adulteries, fornications, thefts, false witness, blasphemies. *Matt. 15:19.*

230 When lust hath conceived, it *bringeth forth sin*. *James 1:15.* (Sins of commission.)

231 To him that *knoweth to do good* and *doeth it not,* to him it is *sin. James 4:17.* (Sins of omission.)

99. Where alone can we find salvation from sin?

We find salvation only *in the Gospel,* which tells us that Christ as our Substitute fulfilled the Law and suffered and died for us.

232 Christ is the end of the Law for righteousness to everyone that believeth. *Rom. 10:4.*

233 *Christ hath redeemed us* from the curse of the Law, being made a *curse for us;* for it is written, Cursed is everyone that hangeth on a tree. *Gal. 3:13.*

The Fall

The Redemption

PART II

The Apostles' Creed

100. What is a creed?

A creed is a *statement of what we believe and teach*.

Bible Narrative: Peter's statement of what the disciples believed. *Matt. 16:13-16.*

101. What is the brief creed in our Catechism called?

It is called the *Apostles' Creed*.

102. Why is it called the Apostles' Creed?

It is called the Apostles' Creed because it is a brief statement of the *teachings, or doctrines, of the Apostles* as found in the Bible.

Creative Hand

THE FIRST ARTICLE

CREATION

I believe in God the Father Almighty, Maker of heaven and earth.

What does this mean? I believe that God has made me and all creatures; that He has given me my body and soul, eyes, ears, and all my members, my reason and all my senses, and still preserves them;

also clothing and shoes, meat and drink, house and home, wife and children, fields, cattle, and all my goods; that He richly and daily provides me with all that I need to support this body and life;

that He defends me against all danger, and guards and protects me from all evil;

and all this purely out of fatherly, divine goodness and mercy, without any merit or worthiness in me;

for all which it is my duty to thank and praise, to serve and obey Him.

This is most certainly true.

I BELIEVE

103. What do you mean when you confess, "I believe in God"?

I mean that I *know, and accept as true,* what the Bible says of God and *trust in Him and rely on Him* with firm confidence.

234   How shall they believe in Him of whom they have not *heard?* Rom. 10:14.

235   So, then, faith cometh *by hearing,* and hearing by the *Word of God.* Rom. 10:17.

236   Faith is the *substance of things hoped for,* the evidence of things *not seen.* Heb. 11:1.

237   I *trusted* in Thee, O Lord; I said, Thou art *my God.* Ps. 31:14.

238   Commit thy way unto the Lord; *trust also in Him;* and He shall bring it to pass. Ps. 37:5.

239   Thou believest that there is one God; thou doest well; the devils also believe — and tremble. *James 2:19.* (Faith of the head and mouth, or dead faith.)

Bible Narratives: The centurion of Capernaum had faith in the Lord. *Luke 7:1-10.* — The nobleman believed the word of the Lord. *John 4:47-53.* — The woman of Canaan trusted in the Lord. *Matt. 15:21-28.*

104. Why do you say in each of the three articles, "I believe," and not, "we believe"?

Everyone must *believe for himself;* no one can be saved by another's faith.

240   The just shall live by *his* faith. Hab. 2:4.

241   *Thy* faith hath saved thee; go in peace. Luke 7:50.

Bible Narrative: The foolish virgins could not obtain oil from the wise virgins. *Matt. 25:8-12.*

105. Why do you here call the First Person of the Trinity "the Father"?

I call Him the Father because He is the *Father of my Lord Jesus Christ* and also *my Father.*

242   I ascend unto *My Father* and *your Father,* and to My God and your God. John 20:17.

243   Have we not *all one Father?*   Hath not one God *created us?* *Mal. 2:10.*

NOTE. — But see *Gal. 3:26.*

244   For this cause I bow my knees unto the *Father of our Lord Jesus Christ,* of whom the *whole family* in heaven and earth is named. *Eph. 3:14, 15.*

GOD MADE ME AND ALL CREATURES

106. Why do you call God "Almighty" and "Maker"?

Creator's Star

I call God "Almighty" and "Maker" because *by His almighty word He made all things out of nothing.*

245   In the beginning God *created* the heaven and the earth. *Gen. 1:1.*

246   Through faith we understand that the worlds were *framed by the word of God,* so that things which are seen were not made of things which do appear. *Heb. 11:3.*

Bible Narrative: Creation. *Gen. 1 and 2.*

107. What do you mean by "heaven and earth"?

By heaven and earth I mean *all creatures,* visible ·and invisible.

247   By Him were *all things* created that are in heaven and that are in earth, *visible and invisible. Col. 1:16.*

THE ANGELS

108. Which are the foremost invisible creatures?

The *angels* are the foremost invisible creatures.

109. How many kinds of angels are there?

There are *two kinds* of angels, *good and evil.*

110. What does the Bible tell us about the good angels?

The Bible tells us that the good angels —

A. Are *holy spirits* confirmed in their bliss;

248   Are they not all ministering *spirits*, sent forth to minister for them who shall be heirs of salvation? *Heb. 1:14.*

249a   When the Son of Man shall come in His glory and all the *holy angels* with Him, then shall He sit upon the throne of His glory. *Matt. 25:31.*

249b   In heaven their angels do *always* behold the face of My Father which is *in heaven. Matt. 18:10.*

B. Are of *great number* and *great power;*

250   Suddenly there was with the angel a *multitude* of the heavenly host. *Luke 2:13.*

251   *Thousand thousands* ministered unto Him, and *ten thousand times ten thousand* stood before Him. *Dan. 7:10.*

252   Bless the Lord, ye His angels, that *excel in strength. Ps. 103:20.*

Bible Narratives: One angel slew 185,000 of Sennacherib's army. *2 Kings 19:35.* — Elisha and his servant were protected by the heavenly hosts. *2 Kings 6:15-17.*

C. *Praise God, carry out His commands*, and *serve the Christians*, especially the children.

253   *Bless* the Lord, ye His angels, that excel in strength, that do His commandments, hearkening unto the voice of His word. *Bless* ye the Lord, all ye His hosts; ye ministers of His, that *do His pleasure. Ps. 103:20, 21.*

254   Are they not all *ministering spirits*, sent forth to minister for them who shall be *heirs of salvation? Heb. 1:14.*

²⁵⁵ He shall give His angels *charge over thee* to *keep thee in all thy ways*. They *shall bear thee up* in their hands lest thou dash thy foot against a stone. *Ps. 91:11, 12.*

Bible Narratives: At the birth of Christ the multitude of the heavenly host praised God. *Luke 2:13, 14.* — An angel set Peter free. *Acts 12:5-11.* — An angel shut the lions' mouths and saved Daniel. *Dan. 6.* — Angels carried Lazarus into Abraham's bosom. *Luke 16:22.*

111. What does the Bible tell us about the evil angels, or devils?

The Bible tells us that the evil angels, or devils, —

A. Are *spirits* who were *created holy,* but *sinned* and are forever *rejected* by God;

²⁵⁶ God spared not the *angels that sinned,* but *cast them down to hell* and delivered them into chains of darkness, to be *reserved unto Judgment. 2 Peter 2:4.*

B. Are *cunning, powerful, and of great number;*

²⁵⁷ We wrestle not against flesh and blood, but against *principalities,* against *powers,* against the *rulers of the darkness of this world,* against *spiritual wickedness* in high places. *Eph. 6:12.*

²⁵⁸ He answered, saying, My name is Legion; for *we are many. Mark 5:9.*

NOTE. — See 2 Cor. 11:13, 14.

C. Are *enemies of God and of man and endeavor to destroy the works of God.*

²⁵⁹ [The devil] was a *murderer* from the beginning and abode not in the truth, because there is no truth in him. When he speaketh a lie, he speaketh of his own; for he is a *liar,* and the father of it. *John 8:44.*

260 . Be sober, be vigilant; because your adversary, the devil, as a roaring lion walketh about, *seeking whom he may devour;* whom resist steadfast in the faith. *1 Peter 5:8, 9.*

Bible Narratives: The serpent led Eve into sin. *Gen. 3:1-5.* — Satan sought the destruction of Job. *Job 2.* — The Tempter tried to mislead Jesus. *Matt. 4:1-11.*

MAN

112. Which is the foremost visible creature?

The foremost visible creature is *man,* because in the beginning God Himself especially formed his body, gave him a rational soul, made him ruler over the earth, and, above all, created him in His image.

261 The Lord God *formed* man of the dust of the ground and breathed into his nostrils the *breath of life;* and man became a living soul. *Gen. 2:7.*

262 God said, Let Us make man *in Our image,* after Our likeness; and let them have *dominion* over the fish of the sea and over the fowl of the air and over the cattle and over all the earth and over every creeping thing that creepeth upon the earth. So God created man *in His own image,* in the image of God created He him; male and female created He them. *Gen. 1:26, 27.*

113. What was the image of God?

The image of God consisted in this —

A. That man *knew God* and was *perfectly happy* in such knowledge.

263 [Ye] have put on the new man, which is renewed in *knowledge* after the *image of Him that created him.* *Col. 3:10.*

B. That man was *perfectly holy* and blessed.

264   Put on the new man, which *after God* is created in *righteousness and true holiness.* Eph. 4:24.

114. Does man still bear the image of God?

Man *lost* the image of God when he *fell into sin.* In *believers,* a *beginning* of its renewal is made. Only *in heaven,* however, will this image be *fully* restored.

265   [Adam] begat a son *in his own likeness,* after his image. *Gen. 5:3.*

NOTE. — See 263 and 264.

266   I will *behold Thy face in righteousness;* I shall be satisfied, when I awake, *with Thy likeness. Ps. 17:15.*

115. What do you confess in the explanation of the First Article about your creation?

I believe that God has made *me and all creatures;* that He has given me my *body and soul,* eyes, ears, and all my members, my reason, and all my senses.

267   I will praise Thee; for I am fearfully and *wonderfully made;* marvelous are Thy works; and that my soul knoweth right well. *Ps. 139:14.*

GOD STILL PRESERVES ME AND ALL CREATURES

116. What does God still do for you and all creatures?

He still *preserves* me and all creatures.

268   O Lord, Thou preservest man and beast. *Ps. 36:6.*

269   [He upholds] all things by the word of His power. *Heb. 1:3.*

Hand of Blessing

117. How does God preserve you?

A. He gives me clothing and shoes, meat and drink, house and home, wife and children, fields, cattle, and all my goods; He richly and daily provides me with all that I need to support this body and life. (Preservation.)

270   The eyes of all wait upon Thee; and *Thou givest them their meat in due season*. Thou openest Thine hand and *satisfiest* the desire of every living thing. *Ps. 145:15, 16*.

271   Cast all your care upon Him; for *He careth for you*. *1 Peter 5:7*.

Bible Narratives: God preserved Noah and his descendants. *Gen. 9:1-3*. — God preserved Israel in the wilderness. *Deut. 8:3, 4*. — God preserved Elijah, the widow, and her son during the famine. *1 Kings 17*.

NOTE. — See Psalms 104 and 147.

B. He *defends* me against all danger and *guards and protects* me from all evil. (Government of God.)

272   Are not two sparrows sold for a farthing? And one of them shall not fall on the ground without your Father. But the very *hairs of your head are all numbered*. *Matt. 10:29, 30*.

273   There shall *no evil* befall thee, neither shall any plague come nigh thy dwelling. *Ps. 91:10*.

274   Ye thought *evil against me;* but *God meant it unto good,* to bring to pass, as it is this day, to save much people alive. *Gen. 50:20*.

275   *Commit thy way* unto the Lord; trust also in Him; and He shall bring it to pass. *Ps. 37:5.*

276   My times are in Thy hand. *Ps. 31:15.*

Bible Narratives: God directed Lot to flee to the mountains before the destruction of Sodom. *Gen. 19.* — God delivered Israel from bondage, guided and protected them on their way. *Ex. 13:14.*

118. What moves God to do all this for you?

God does all this purely out of *fatherly, divine goodness and mercy,* without any *merit* or *worthiness* in me.

277   *Like as a father* pitieth his children, so the Lord pitieth them that fear Him. *Ps. 103:13.*

278   I am *not worthy* of the least of all the mercies and of all the truth which Thou hast showed unto Thy servant. *Gen. 32:10.*

Bible Narrative: The centurion of Capernaum confessed that he was not worthy to have the Lord come under his roof. *Luke 7:6, 7.*

119. What, then, do you owe your Father in heaven for all this?

For all this it is my duty to *thank* and *praise,* to *serve* and *obey* Him.

279   *Oh, give thanks* unto the Lord, for He is good; because His mercy endureth forever. *Ps. 118:1.*

280   What shall *I render unto the Lord* for all His benefits toward me? *Ps. 116:12.*

120. Why do you close this article with the words "This is most certainly true"?

Because all that I confess in this article is plainly taught in the Bible; therefore I firmly believe it.

THE SECOND ARTICLE

REDEMPTION

~~I~~ *and* believe in Jesus Christ, His only Son, our Lord, who was conceived by the Holy Ghost *Spirit*, born of the Virgin Mary, suffered under Pontius Pilate, was crucified, dead *died*, and buried;

He descended into hell; the third day He rose again from the dead; He ascended into heaven, and sitteth on the right hand of God the Father Almighty; from thence He shall come to judge the quick *living* and the dead.

What does this mean? I believe that Jesus Christ, true God, begotten of the Father from eternity, and also true man, born of the Virgin Mary, is my Lord,

who has redeemed me, a lost and condemned creature, purchased and won me from all sins, from death, and from the power of the devil; not with gold or silver, but with His holy, precious blood and with His innocent suffering and death, that I may be His own and live under Him in His kingdom, and serve Him in everlasting righteousness, innocence, and blessedness,

even as He is risen from the dead, lives and reigns to all eternity.

This is most certainly true.

THE NAMES JESUS AND CHRIST

121. Of whom does this article treat?

This article treats of *Jesus Christ*.

122. Why is He called Jesus?

He is called Jesus because He is the *only Savior* of all mankind.

Je(su)s

281 She shall bring forth a Son, and thou shalt call His name *Jesus;* for He shall *save* His people from their sins. *Matt. 1:21.*

282 Neither is there salvation in any other; for there is *none other name* under heaven given among men whereby we must be *saved*. *Acts 4:12.*

123. Why is He called Christ?

He is called Christ, or the Messiah (as foretold in Old Testament prophecy), that is, the Anointed, because He has been *anointed with the Holy Ghost* without measure.

Chr(ist)

283   God, Thy God, hath *anointed Thee* with the Oil of Gladness above Thy fellows. *Ps. 45:7.*

284   God *anointed Jesus of Nazareth* with the *Holy Ghost* and with power. *Acts 10:38.*

285   God giveth not the Spirit by measure unto Him [Christ]. *John 3:34.*

NOTE. — Other names for Jesus Christ are: Lord, John 20:28; Redeemer, Is. 59:20; Savior, Luke 2:11; The Word, John 1:14; Son of God, Matt. 16:16; Son of Man, Matt. 25:31; Angel of God (Old Testament), Ex. 14:19; Emmanuel, Matt. 1:23.

124. What do you mean when you confess, I believe in Jesus Christ?

I know and accept the *Christ* of the Bible *as my personal Savior* and *trust only in Him* for my salvation.

286   This is life eternal that they might *know* Thee the only true God, and *Jesus Christ*, whom Thou hast sent. *John 17:3.*

287   He that *believeth not* the Son shall *not see life*, but the wrath of God abideth on him. *John 3:36.*

288   *I know* whom I have believed and am persuaded that He is able to keep that which I have committed unto Him against that Day. *2 Tim. 1:12.*

THE TWO NATURES IN JESUS CHRIST

125. Who is Jesus Christ?

Jesus Christ is *true God*, begotten of the Father from eternity, and also *true man*, born of the Virgin Mary.

126. Why do you believe that Jesus Christ is true God?

I believe that Jesus Christ is true God because the Scriptures ascribe to Him —

A. *Divine names;*

289   This is the *true God* and eternal *Life. 1 John 5:20.*

290   Thomas answered and said unto Him, *My Lord and my God. John 20:28.*

291   Behold, a voice out of the cloud, which said, This is *My beloved Son,* in whom I am well pleased; hear ye Him. *Matt. 17:5.*

292   Christ came, who is over all, God blessed forever. *Rom. 9:5.*

Christ, Alpha and Omega

B. *Divine attributes;*

293   *In the beginning was* the Word, and the Word was with God, and the Word was God. The same *was in the beginning with God. John 1:1, 2.* (Eternity.)

294   Jesus Christ *the same yesterday and today and forever. Heb. 13:8.* (Unchangeableness.)

295   Lo, I am *with you alway,* even unto the end of the world. *Matt. 28:20.* (Omnipresence.)

Note. — See Matt. 18:20.

296   Lord, Thou *knowest all things. John 21:17.* (Omniscience.)

297   *All power* is given unto Me in heaven and in earth. *Matt. 28:18.* (Omnipotence.)

Bible Narratives: Jesus knows the name and character of Nathanael. *John 1:48.* — Jesus and the woman at Jacob's Well. *John 4:17, 18.* — Miraculous draught of fishes. *Luke 5: 4-6; John 21:6.*

Note.—See also Matt. 21:1-7; Luke 22:8-13; Matt. 26:20-25; Luke 18:31-33.

c. *Divine works;*

298 All things *were made by Him;* and without Him was not anything made that was made. *John 1:3.* (Creation.)

299 [He *upholds*] all things by the word of His power. *Heb. 1:3.* (Preservation.)

300 The Son of Man hath *power* on earth to *forgive sins.* *Matt. 9:6.*

301 [The Father] hath given Him authority *to execute judgment.* *John 5:27.*

Bible Narratives: At the marriage feast in Cana, Jesus manifested His glory by turning water into wine. *John 2:1-11.* — He rebuked the storm. *Luke 8:22-25.* — He healed the man sick of the palsy. *Matt. 9:1-8.* — He called Lazarus back to life. *John 11:38-44.* — He rose from the dead. *Matt. 28:6, 7.*

d. *Divine honor and glory.*

302 All men should *honor the Son even as they honor the Father.* He that honoreth not the Son honoreth not the Father, which hath sent Him. *John 5:23.*

303 Let all the angels of God *worship Him. Heb. 1:6.*

Note. — See Phil. 2:10; Rev. 5:12, 13.

127. Why do you believe that Jesus Christ is also true man?

I believe that Jesus Christ is also true man because the Scriptures —

a. *Expressly call Him man;*

304 There is one God and one Mediator between God and men, the *man Christ Jesus. 1 Tim. 2:5.*

b. *Ascribe to Him a human body and soul;*

305 Behold My *hands* and My *feet,* that it is I Myself; handle Me and see; for a spirit hath not *flesh* and *bones,* as ye see Me have. *Luke 24:39.*

306 *My soul* is exceeding sorrowful, even unto death. *Matt. 26:38.*

c. *Ascribe to Him human feelings and actions.*

Bible Narratives: Jesus slept. *Mark 4:38.* — Jesus hungered. *Matt. 4:2.* — Jesus thirsted. *John 19:28.* — Jesus wept. *John 11:35.* — Jesus suffered and died. *Matt. 26 and 27.*

128. What two natures, then, are united in Christ?

The *divine* and the *human* natures are united in Christ, *both natures together forming one undivided and indivisible person* (personal union).

307 *The Word was made flesh* and dwelt among us (and we beheld His glory, the glory as of the Only-begotten of the Father), full of grace and truth. *John 1:14.*

308 Without controversy great is the mystery of godliness: *God was manifest in the flesh. 1 Tim. 3:16.*

309 In Him dwelleth all the *fullness of the Godhead bodily. Col. 2:9.*

310 Unto us a *Child is born,* unto us a Son is given; and the government shall be upon His shoulder; and His name shall be called Wonderful, Counselor, *The Mighty God, The Everlasting Father,* The Prince of Peace. *Is. 9:6.*

311 *All power* is given unto Me in heaven and in earth. *Matt. 28:18.*

312 Lo, *I am with you alway,* even unto the end of the world. *Matt. 28:20.*

313 [Ye] *killed the Prince of Life. Acts 3:15.*

314 The *blood* of Jesus Christ, *His Son, cleanseth* us from all sin. *1 John 1:7.*

129. Why was it necessary for our Savior to be true man?

It was necessary for our Savior to be true man —

A. That He might *take our place under the Law;*

315   When the fullness of the time was come, God sent forth His Son, made of a woman, *made under the Law,* to *redeem them that were under the Law,* that we might receive the adoption of sons. *Gal. 4:4, 5.*

B. That He might be able to *suffer and die in our stead.*

316   Forasmuch, then, as the children are partakers of flesh and blood, He also Himself likewise took part of the same, that *through death* He might destroy him that had the power of death, that is, the devil. *Heb. 2:14.*

130. Why was it necessary for our Savior to be true God?

It was necessary for our Savior to be true God —

A. That His fulfilling of the Law might be sufficient for all men;

317   None of them can by any means redeem his brother nor give to God a ransom for him. For the redemption of their soul is precious. *Ps. 49:7, 8.*

318   By the obedience of one shall many be made righteous. *Rom. 5:19.*

B. That *His life* and *death* might be a *sufficient ransom* for our redemption.

319   The Son of Man came, not to be ministered unto, but to minister and to give His *life a ransom* for many. *Mark 10:45.*

c. That He might be able to *overcome death and the devil* for us.

320   Christ hath abolished *death. 2 Tim. 1:10.*

321   Forasmuch, then, as the children are partakers of flesh and blood, He also Himself likewise took part of the same, that through death He might *destroy him that had the power of death,* that is, *the devil. Heb. 2:14.*

322   Thanks be to God, which giveth us the *victory through our Lord Jesus Christ. 1 Cor. 15:57.*

131. What do you confess of the God-man Jesus Christ?

I believe that Jesus Christ is *my Lord* and Redeemer.

THE OFFICE OF CHRIST

132. For what threefold office was Christ anointed?

Christ was anointed to be my *Prophet, Priest,* and *King.*

A. As my *Prophet,* He *revealed Himself* by word and deed, and *by the preaching of the Gospel* still *reveals Himself* as the *Son of God* and the *Redeemer* of the world.

323   The Lord, thy God, will raise up unto thee a *Prophet* from the midst of thee, of thy brethren, like unto me; *unto Him ye shall hearken. Deut. 18:15.*

324   This is My beloved Son, in whom I am well pleased; *hear ye Him. Matt. 17:5.*

325   The Law was given by Moses, but *grace and truth came by Jesus Christ.* No man hath seen God at any time; the only-begotten Son, which is in the bosom of the Father, *He hath declared Him. John 1:17, 18.*

326   *He that heareth you heareth Me;* and he that despiseth you despiseth Me; and he that despiseth Me despiseth Him that sent Me. *Luke 10:16.*

B. As my *Priest,* Christ *fulfilled the Law* in my stead perfectly (active obedience), *sacrificed Himself* for me (passive obedience), and still *intercedes* (pleads) for me with His heavenly Father.

Lamb of God

327   When the fullness of the time was come, God sent forth His Son, made of a woman, *made under the Law,* to *redeem them that were under the Law,* that we might receive the adoption of sons. *Gal. 4:4, 5.*

328   Christ *died for our sins* according to the Scriptures. *1 Cor. 15:3.*

329   Such an *High Priest* became us who is holy, harmless, undefiled, separate from sinners, and made higher than the heavens; who needeth not daily, as those high priests, to offer up sacrifice, first for His own sins and then for the people's; for *this He did once when He offered up Himself. Heb. 7:26, 27.*

330   If any man sin, we have an *Advocate* with the Father, Jesus Christ, the Righteous; and He is the Propitiation for our sins; and not for ours only, but also for the sins of the whole world. *1 John 2:1, 2.*

C. As my *King,* Christ with His almighty power *rules over all creatures, governs and protects His Church,* and finally *leads it to glory.*

331   *All power* is given unto Me *in heaven and in earth. Matt. 28:18.* (The Kingdom of Power. — All creatures.)

332   Jesus answered, My kingdom is not of this world. If
My kingdom were of this world, then would My servants fight
that I should not be delivered to the Jews. But now is My
kingdom not from hence. Pilate therefore said unto Him, Art
Thou a king, then? Jesus answered, Thou sayest that *I am
a king*. To this end was I born, and for this cause came
I into the world, that I should *bear witness unto the truth*.
Everyone that *is of the truth heareth My voice*. *John 18:
36, 37*. (The Kingdom of Grace. — The Church on earth.)
NOTE. — See Matt. 16:18.

333   The Lord shall *deliver* me from every evil work and
will *preserve me unto His heavenly kingdom;* to whom be
glory forever and ever. Amen. *2 Tim. 4:18*. (The Kingdom
of Glory. — The Church in heaven.)

133. What two states do we distinguish in Christ's work of redemption?

The *State of Humiliation* and the *State of
Exaltation.*

THE SAVIOR IN THE STATE OF HUMILIATION

134. Wherein did Christ's State of Humiliation consist?

Christ's State of Humiliation consisted in
this, that according to His *human* nature, Christ
did *not always* and *not fully use* the divine attributes *communicated* to His human nature.

334   Let this mind be in you which was also in Christ Jesus,
who, being *in the form of God*, thought it not robbery to be
equal with God; but made Himself of *no reputation* and
took upon Him the *form of a servant* and was made in the
likeness of men; and being found in *fashion as a man*, He
humbled Himself and became *obedient unto death*, even the
death *of the cross*. *Phil. 2:5-8*.

Bible Narratives: John 2:11. John 11:40. John 18:6. (Rays
of hidden glory.)

135. In what words does the Second Article describe the State of Humiliation?

"Conceived by the Holy Ghost; born of the Virgin Mary; suffered under Pontius Pilate; was crucified, dead, and buried."

136. What do the Scriptures teach of the conception of Christ?

The Scriptures teach that by the miraculous working of the Holy Ghost, Christ, the Son of God, received His human body and soul in the Virgin Mary.

335 The *Holy Ghost* shall come upon thee, and the *power of the Highest* shall overshadow thee; therefore also that *Holy Thing which shall be born* of thee shall be called the Son of God. *Luke 1:35.*

336 Joseph, thou son of David, fear not to take unto thee Mary, thy wife; for that which is *conceived* in her is of the *Holy Ghost. Matt. 1:20.*

137. What do the Scriptures teach of the birth of Christ?

The Nativity
Christmas Rose

The Scriptures teach that Christ was born of the Virgin Mary a *true man.*

337 Behold, a *virgin* shall conceive and bear a Son and shall call His name Immanuel. *Is. 7:14.* (Virgin Birth. — Matt. 1:18.)

338 Unto us a Child is *born,* unto us a Son is given. *Is. 9:6.*

339 She brought forth her first-born Son and wrapped Him in swaddling clothes and laid Him in a manger, because there was no room for them in the inn. *Luke 2:7.*

138. What do the Scriptures teach of the suffering and death of Christ?

The Scriptures teach that —

A. In *His earthly life* Christ suffered *poverty, contempt,* and *persecution;*

340   Though He was rich, yet for your sakes He became *poor,* that ye through *His poverty* might be rich. *2 Cor. 8:9.*

341   The foxes have holes, and the birds of the air have nests; but the Son of Man *hath not where to lay His head. Matt. 8:20.*

342   He is *despised and rejected* of men; a man of sorrows and acquainted with grief; and we hid, as it were, our faces from Him; He was *despised,* and we esteemed Him not. *Is. 53:3.*

343   *Ye seek to kill Me,* a man that hath told you the truth, which I have heard of God. *John 8:40.*

Bible Narratives: At His birth Jesus had only swaddling clothes and a manger. *Luke 2:7.* — Herod sought to destroy Him; flight to Egypt. *Matt. 2:13.* — In Nazareth the Jews tried to cast Him down from the brow of the hill. *Luke 4:29.* — In the Temple they took up stones to throw at Him. *John 8:59.*

B. *Under Pontius Pilate,* Christ suffered extreme *agony of body and soul;*

344   Pilate therefore took Jesus and *scourged* Him. And the soldiers platted a crown of thorns and put it on His head; and they put on Him a purple robe and said, Hail, King of the Jews! And they *smote* Him with their hands. *John 19:1-3.*

345   Then delivered he Him therefore unto them *to be crucified.* And they took Jesus and led Him away. And He, *bearing His cross,* went forth into a place called the place of a skull, which is called in the Hebrew Golgotha, where they *crucified Him. John 19:16-18.*

NOTE. — See Ps. 22:6-8, 14-16; Ps. 69:17-21.

346   About the ninth hour Jesus cried with a loud voice, saying . . . My God, My God, why hast *Thou forsaken* Me? *Matt. 27:46.* (He suffered the tortures of the damned in hell.)

c. Christ *died* on the accursed tree of the cross.

347   He bowed His head and *gave up the ghost. John 19:30.*

348   It is written, *Cursed* is everyone that hangeth on a tree. *Gal. 3:13.*

139. What do the Scriptures teach of the burial of Christ?

Christ's body was *laid in the* grave and remained there to the third day, but *without seeing corruption,* or decay.

349   He whom God raised again *saw no corruption. Acts 13:37.*

CHRIST'S WORK OF REDEMPTION, OR ATONEMENT

140. For what purpose did Christ so humble Himself?

Christ so humbled Himself *to redeem me,* a lost and condemned creature.

141. From what has Christ redeemed you?

Christ has redeemed me from *all sins,* from *death,* and from the *power of the devil.*

142. How has Christ redeemed you from all sins?

A. Christ has *taken away all my guilt* and *suffered all my punishment.*

350 By the obedience of One shall many be made righteous.
Rom. 5:19.

351 He hath made Him to be *sin for us* who knew no sin,
that we might be made the righteousness of God in Him.
2 Cor. 5:21.

352 Behold the Lamb of God, which *taketh away the sin*
of the world. *John 1:29.*

353 Christ hath *redeemed us from the curse* of the Law,
being made a curse for us; for it is written, Cursed is everyone that hangeth on a tree. *Gal. 3:13.*

B. Christ has *freed me from the slavery of sin.*

354 [Christ] His own self bare our sins in His own body on
the tree, that we, being *dead to sins,* should *live unto righteousness;* by whose stripes ye were healed. *1 Peter 2:24.*

355 Verily, verily, I say unto you, Whosoever committeth
sin is the servant of sin. If the Son therefore shall make
you free, ye shall be free indeed. *John 8:34, 36.*

143. How has Christ redeemed you from death?

Christ has overcome death; now I need *not
fear temporal death,* since *eternal death has no
power* over me.

356 Forasmuch, then, as the children are partakers of flesh
and blood, He also Himself likewise took part of the same
that through death He *might destroy him that had the power
of death,* that is, the devil, and *deliver them* who through
fear of death were all their lifetime subject to bondage.
Heb. 2:14, 15.

357 O death, *where is thy sting?* O grave, where is *thy
victory?* The sting of death is sin, and the strength of sin is
the Law. But thanks be to God, which giveth *us* the victory
through our Lord Jesus Christ. *1 Cor. 15:55-57.*

358 Our Savior, Jesus Christ . . . hath *abolished death* and
hath brought *life and immortality* to light. *2 Tim. 1:10.*

144. How has Christ redeemed you from the power of the devil?

Christ has *overcome* the devil and *conquered* him; therefore he can no longer successfully *accuse me*, and I can now overcome his temptations.

359   I will put enmity between thee and the woman, and between thy seed and her Seed. It shall *bruise thy head,* and thou shalt bruise His heel. *Gen. 3:15.*

360   For this purpose the Son of God was manifested, that He might *destroy the works of the devil. 1 John 3:8.*

361   Resist the devil, and he *will flee* from you. *James 4:7.* NOTE. — See 356. — See also Col. 2:15; Rom. 8:31-34; Rev. 12:10; and 1 Peter 5:8, 9.

145. With what has Christ redeemed you?

Christ has redeemed me, not with gold or silver, but with His *holy, precious blood* and with His *innocent suffering and death.*

362   Ye know that ye were not redeemed with corruptible things, as silver and gold, from your vain conversation received by tradition from your fathers, but with the *precious blood of Christ,* as of a lamb without blemish and without spot. *1 Peter 1:18, 19.*

363   The *blood* of Jesus Christ, His Son, *cleanseth us* from all sin. *1 John 1:7.*

364   With *His stripes* we are healed. *Is. 53:5.*

146. How does this work of redemption benefit you?

As my *Substitute* Christ has *atoned,* or made satisfaction, for my sins by *paying the penalty* of my guilt. (Vicarious Atonement.)

365 He hath made Him to be *sin for us* who knew no sin, that we might be made the *righteousness* of God *in Him*. *2 Cor. 5:21.*

366 Surely He hath borne *our* griefs and carried *our* sorrows; yet we did esteem Him stricken, smitten of God, and afflicted. But He was *wounded for our transgressions*, He was *bruised for our iniquities;* the chastisement of our peace was upon Him; and *with His stripes we are healed*. *Is. 53:4, 5.*

147. Has Christ redeemed, purchased, and won only you?

Christ has redeemed *me and all lost and condemned mankind*.

367 This is a faithful saying and worthy of all acceptation, that Christ Jesus came into the world to save *sinners;* of whom I am chief. *1 Tim. 1:15.*

368 The Son of Man is come to save *that which was lost*. *Matt. 18:11.*

369 Behold the Lamb of God, which taketh away the sin of the *world*. *John 1:29.*

370 He is the Propitiation for our sins; and *not for ours only*, but also for the sins *of the whole world*. *1 John 2:2.*

371 He died for *all*. *2 Cor. 5:15.*

372 [They *deny*] the Lord that *bought them* and bring upon themselves swift destruction. *2 Peter 2:1.*

THE SAVIOR IN THE STATE OF EXALTATION

148. Wherein does Christ's State of Exaltation consist?

Christ's State of Exaltation consists in this, that according to His *human* nature, Christ *always and fully uses* the divine attributes *communicated* to His human nature.

373   God also *hath highly exalted Him* and given Him a name which is above every name, that at the name of Jesus every knee should bow, of things in heaven and things in earth and things under the earth, and that every tongue should confess that Jesus Christ is Lord, to the glory of God the Father. *Phil. 2:9-11.*

149. In what words does the Second Article speak of the State of Exaltation?

"He descended into hell; the third day He rose again from the dead; He ascended into heaven and sitteth on the right hand of God the Father Almighty; from thence He shall come to judge the quick and the dead."

150. What do the Scriptures teach of Christ's descent into hell?

The Scriptures teach that Christ, having been *made alive* in His grave, descended into hell, not to suffer, but to *proclaim His victory over His enemies.*

374   [Christ was] put to death in the flesh, but quickened by the spirit; by which also *He went and preached* unto the spirits in prison. *1 Peter 3:18, 19.*

151. What do the Scriptures teach of Christ's resurrection?

Easter Cross

The Scriptures teach that on the third day Christ victoriously *rose from the grave* and *showed Himself alive* to His disciples.

375   Him God raised up the <u>third day</u> and *showed Him openly;* not to all the people, but unto *witnesses* chosen before of God, even to us, who did *eat and drink with Him after He rose from the dead. Acts 10:40, 41.*

376   He rose again the *third day* according to the Scriptures; and . . . was *seen of Cephas,* then of the *Twelve;* after that He was seen of above *five hundred* brethren at once, of whom the greater part remain unto this present, but some are fallen asleep. After that He was seen of *James,* then of *all the Apostles.* And last of all He was seen of *me also,* as of one born out of due time. *1 Cor. 15:4-8.*

377   To whom also He *showed Himself alive* after His Passion by many infallible proofs, being seen of them *forty days* and *speaking* of the things pertaining to the kingdom of God. *Acts 1:3.*

Bible Narrative: The narrative of Christ's resurrection. *Matt. 27:62-66; Matt. 28. — Mark 16. — Luke 24. — John 20 and 21.*

152. Why is the resurrection of Christ of such importance and comfort to us?

Christ's resurrection *definitely proves* —

A: That Christ is the *Son of God;*

378   [He was] *declared* to be the *Son of God* with *power,* according to the spirit of holiness, *by the resurrection* from the dead. *Rom. 1:4.*

B. That His *doctrine is the truth;*

379 Destroy this temple, and in three days I will raise it up.
John 2:19.

C. That God the *Father has accepted* the
sacrifice of His Son for the reconciliation of
the world;

380 If Christ be *not raised,* your *faith is vain;* ye are *yet in
your sins.* *1 Cor. 15:17.*

381 [Christ] was delivered for our offenses and was *raised
again for our justification.* *Rom. 4:25.*

D. That all believers shall *rise unto eternal life.*

382 Because I live, ye shall *live also.* *John 14:19.*

383 I am the Resurrection and the Life. He *that believeth*
in Me, though he were dead, yet *shall he live;* and whosoever
liveth and *believeth in Me shall never die.* *John 11:25, 26.*

**153. What do the Scriptures teach of Christ's
ascension into heaven?**

The Scriptures teach that, according to His
human nature, Christ *visibly* ascended to heaven
and entered *into the glory* of His Father, as our
Forerunner. (Heb. 6:20.)

384 He that descended is the same also that ascended up
far *above all heavens.* *Eph. 4:10.*

385 Father, I will that they also whom Thou hast given
Me *be with Me where I am,* that they may behold My glory.
John 17:24.

386 I will *come again* and receive *you unto Myself,* that
where *I am,* there *ye may be* also. *John 14:3.*

Bible Narrative: The narrative of Christ's ascension. *Luke
24:50, 51. — Acts 1:9-11.*

154. What do the Scriptures teach of Christ's sitting on the right hand of God the Father Almighty?

The Scriptures teach that Christ, also according to His *human* nature, *rules and fills* all things with *divine power* and *majesty*.

387 [God] set Him [Christ] at His own *right hand* in the heavenly places, far above all principality and power and might and dominion and every name that is named, not only in this world, but also in that which is to come; and hath put *all things under His feet* and gave Him to be the Head over all things to the Church, which is His body, the fullness of Him that *filleth all in all*. *Eph. 1:20-23.*

155. What comfort do you derive from Christ's sitting on the right hand of God?

We derive the comfort that it is the *exalted* Christ who —

A. As our *Prophet sends men* to preach the Gospel of redemption;

388 [He] ascended up far above all heavens that He might fill all things. And *He gave* some, apostles; and some, prophets; and some, evangelists; and some, *pastors and teachers*; for the perfecting of the saints, for the *work of the ministry*, for the edifying of the body of Christ. *Eph. 4:10-12.*

NOTE. — See Luke 10:16.

B. As our *Priest intercedes* (pleads) for us before God;

389 If any man sin, we have an *Advocate* with the Father, Jesus Christ the Righteous. *1 John 2:1.*

390 [Christ] is even at the right hand of God, who also *maketh intercession* for us. *Rom. 8:34.*

c. As our *King governs and protects His Church* and as Head of the Church *rules the world in the interest* of the Church.

NOTE. — See Eph. 1:20-23. See 387.

391   The Lord said unto my Lord, Sit Thou on My *right hand* till I make Thine *enemies Thy footstool. Matt. 22:44; Ps. 110:1.*

156. What do the Scriptures teach of Christ's coming to Judgment?

The Scriptures teach that —

A. Christ will return *visibly* and in *glory;*

392   This same Jesus which is taken up from you into heaven shall so come in like manner as ye have *seen* Him *go* into heaven. *Acts 1:11.*

393   Behold, He cometh with clouds; and *every eye shall see Him,* and they also which pierced Him. *Rev. 1:7.*

394   When the Son of Man shall come in His glory, and all the holy angels with Him, then shall He sit upon the *throne of His glory. Matt. 25:31.*

B. He will then *judge* the world in righteousness by His Word;

395   [He is] ordained of God to be the *Judge* of quick and dead. *Acts 10:42.*

396   We must all appear before the *judgment seat of Christ* that everyone may receive the things done in his body, according to that he hath done, whether it be good or bad. *2 Cor. 5:10.*

397   He will judge the world *in righteousness* by that Man whom He hath ordained. *Acts 17:31.*

398   The *Word* that I have spoken, the same *shall judge* him in the Last Day. *John 12:48.*

c. He will come on the *Last Day*, which is *appointed by God*, but *unknown to man*.

399 [God] hath *appointed* a day in the which He will judge the world. *Acts 17:31.*

400 Of that day and that *hour knoweth no man*, no, not the angels which are in heaven, neither the Son, but the *Father*. *Mark 13:32.*

401 The day of the Lord will come *as a thief in the night*, in the which the heavens shall pass away with a great noise, and the elements shall melt with fervent heat; the earth also and the works that are therein shall be burned up. *2 Peter 3:10.*

402 As the lightning cometh out of the east and shineth even unto the west, so shall also the coming of the Son of Man be. *Matt. 24:27.*

403 *The end* of all things is *at hand*. *1 Peter 4:7.*

Bible Narratives: The final Judgment. *Matt. 25:31-46.* — Signs preceding Christ's coming. *Matt. 24* and *2 Thess. 2.*

157. What is the purpose of Christ's entire work of redemption?

The purpose of Christ's entire work of redemption is —

✳ A. That I may be His own; that is, I am now righteous and blameless in the sight of God.

404 Thou wast slain and hast redeemed us *to God* by Thy blood. *Rev. 5:9.*

405 Ye are not your own. *1 Cor. 6:19.*

B. That I may live under Him in His kingdom, and serve Him in everlasting righteousness, innocence, and blessedness; that is, *that I willingly serve Him* by an active Christian life and *enjoy His blessings,* now *on earth* and hereafter *in heaven.*

406   I am crucified with Christ; nevertheless I live; yet not I, but *Christ liveth in me;* and the life which I now live in the flesh I live by the faith of the Son of God, who loved me and gave Himself for me. *Gal. 2:20.*

407   That we, being delivered out of the hand of our enemies, might serve Him without fear, in *holiness* and *righteousness* before Him, all the days of our life. *Luke 1:74, 75.*

408   He died for all that they which live should *not henceforth live unto themselves,* but *unto Him* which died for them and rose again. *2 Cor. 5:15.*

409   We are His workmanship, created in Christ Jesus unto good works, which God hath before ordained that we should walk in them. *Eph. 2:10.*

NOTE. — See Luke 1:67-75; Rom. 12:4-16.

158. Are you sure of your redemption by Christ?

Yes indeed; for my redemption is *as sure as He is risen from the dead, lives and reigns to all eternity.*

159. Why do you close this article with the words "This is most certainly true"?

Because all that I confess in this article is plainly taught in the Bible; therefore I firmly believe it.

**Rock
of Salvation**

THE THIRD ARTICLE

SANCTIFICATION

I believe in the Holy Ghost; the holy Christian Church, the communion of saints; the forgiveness of sins; the resurrection of the body; and the life everlasting. Amen.

What does this mean? I believe that I cannot by my own reason or strength believe in Jesus Christ, my Lord, or come to Him; but the Holy Ghost has called me by the Gospel, enlightened me with His gifts, sanctified and kept me in the true faith;

even as He calls, gathers, enlightens, and sanctifies the whole Christian Church on earth, and keeps it with Jesus Christ in the one true faith;

in which Christian Church He daily and richly forgives all sins to me and all believers,

and will at the Last Day raise up me and all the dead, and give unto me and all believers in Christ eternal life.

This is most certainly true.

160. Of what five points does this article treat?

    I. Of the Holy Ghost.

  II. Of the Church, or the Communion of Saints.

 III. Of the Forgiveness of Sins.

 IV. Of the Resurrection of the Body.

  V. Of the Life Everlasting.

I. THE HOLY GHOST

The Person of the Holy Ghost

161. Who is the Holy Ghost?

The Holy Ghost is the *Third Person in the Holy Trinity,* true God with the Father and the Son.

410   Go ye, therefore, and teach all nations, baptizing them in the name of the *Father* and of the *Son* and of the *Holy Ghost. Matt. 28:19.*

Note. — Other names for the Holy Ghost are: Spirit, Spirit of God, 1 Cor. 2:10, 11; Comforter, John 14:26.

162. Why do you believe that the Holy Ghost is true God?

I believe that the Holy Ghost is true God because the Scriptures ascribe to Him —

    A. *Divine names;*

411   Know ye not that ye are the *temple of God* and that the *Spirit of God* dwelleth in you? *1 Cor. 3:16.*

412   Peter said, Ananias, why hath Satan filled thine heart to lie to the *Holy Ghost?* Thou hast not lied unto men, but unto *God. Acts 5:3, 4.*

B. *Divine attributes;*

413 Whither shall I go from Thy *Spirit,* or whither shall I flee from *Thy presence?* If I ascend up into *heaven, Thou art there;* if I make my bed in *hell,* behold, Thou *art there.* If I take the wings of the morning and dwell in the *uttermost parts of the sea, even there* shall Thy hand lead me, and Thy right hand shall hold me. *Ps. 139:7-10.* (Omnipresence.)

414 The Spirit *searcheth all things,* yea, the deep things of God. *1 Cor. 2:10.* (Omniscience.)

415 Christ, who through the *eternal Spirit* offered Himself without spot to God, purge your conscience from dead works to serve the living God. *Heb. 9:14.* (Eternity.)

NOTE. — See Matt. 28:19. (Holiness.)

C. *Divine works;*

416 By the word of the Lord were the heavens made and all the host of them by the *Breath* [Spirit] of His mouth. *Ps. 33:6.* (Creation.)

417 He saved us by the washing of *regeneration* and *renewing* of the *Holy Ghost. Titus 3:5.* (Sanctification.)

D. *Divine honor and glory.*

418 The *Spirit of Glory* and of God resteth upon you. *1 Peter 4:14.*

**The Sevenfold
Gifts of the
Holy Ghost**

THE WORK OF THE HOLY GHOST

163. What is the work of the Holy Ghost?

The Holy Ghost sanctifies me, that is, He *makes me holy,* by bringing me to faith in Christ and by imparting to me the blessings of redemption. (Sanctification in the wider sense includes everything that the Holy Ghost does in me.)

419   But ye are washed, but ye are *sanctified*, but ye are justified in the name of the Lord Jesus and *by the Spirit of our God. 1 Cor. 6:11.*

164. Why is it necessary that the Holy Ghost work this faith in you?

According to the Scriptures I am by nature *spiritually blind, dead,* and an *enemy of God;* therefore I cannot by my own reason or strength believe in Jesus Christ, my Lord, or come to Him.

420   The natural man *receiveth not* the things of the Spirit of God; for they are *foolishness* unto him; *neither can he know* them, because they are spiritually discerned. *1 Cor. 2:14.*

421   [You] were *dead* in trespasses and sins. *Eph. 2:1.*

422   The carnal mind is *enmity* against God. *Rom. 8:7.*

423   By grace are ye saved, through faith, and that *not of yourselves;* it is the gift of God; *not of works,* lest any man should boast. *Eph. 2:8, 9.*

424   No man can say that Jesus is the Lord but *by the Holy Ghost. 1 Cor. 12:3.*

165. What has the Holy Ghost done to bring you to Christ and thus to sanctify you?

The Holy Ghost has *called me by the Gospel,* that is, He has invited me to partake of Christ's blessings, which are offered to me in the Gospel.

425   He *called* you by our Gospel. *2 Thess. 2:14.*

426 [God] hath saved us and *called us* with an holy calling, not according to our works, but according to His own purpose and *grace,* which was given us in Christ Jesus before the world began. *2 Tim. 1:9.*

427 The *Spirit* and the bride say, *Come.* And let him that heareth say, Come. And let him that is athirst come. And whosoever will, let him take the water of life freely. *Rev. 22:17.*

Bible Narratives: Invitation to the great supper. *Luke 14: 16, 17.* — Invitation to the marriage of the king's son. *Matt. 22:1-10.*

166. What did the Holy Ghost work in you when He called you by the Gospel?

By the Gospel the Holy Ghost *enlightened me with* His gifts, that is, He *gave me the saving knowledge of Jesus,* my Savior, so that I *trust* and *believe, rejoice* and *take comfort,* in Him.

428 Ye are a chosen generation, a royal priesthood, an holy nation, a peculiar people, that ye should show forth the praises of Him who hath *called you out of darkness into His marvelous light. 1 Peter 2:9.*

429 God, who commanded the light to shine out of darkness, hath *shined in our hearts to give* the light of the *knowledge* of the glory of God in the face of Jesus Christ. *2 Cor. 4:6.*

430 In whom [Christ], though now ye see Him not, yet *believing,* ye *rejoice* with joy unspeakable. *1 Peter 1:8.*

431 The God of hope fill you with all joy and *peace* in *believing,* that ye may abound in hope through the power of the Holy Ghost. *Rom. 15:13.*

Bible Narratives: The Samaritans were filled with great joy when Philip preached Christ to them. *Acts 8:5-8.* — The jailer at Philippi rejoiced, believing with all his house. *Acts 16:25-34.*

167. What is this work of the Holy Spirit called?

This work of the Holy Spirit is called *conversion*, or *regeneration* (new birth).

432   Turn *Thou me*, and *I shall be turned;* for Thou art the Lord, my God. *Jer. 31:18.* (Conversion.)

433   Jesus answered, Verily, verily, I say unto thee, Except a man be *born* of water and of the *Spirit,* he cannot enter into the kingdom of God. That which is born of the flesh is flesh; and that which is born of the Spirit is spirit. *John 3:5, 6.* (Regeneration.)

168. Why do you say that the Holy Ghost has done this in you by the Gospel?

The Gospel is the *means* whereby the Holy Ghost *offers* us the blessings of Christ and *works* in our hearts that faith by which we accept Christ and His salvation.

NOTE. — The written and spoken Word of God and the Sacraments are the means of grace.

434   Faith cometh by hearing. *Rom. 10:17.*

435   In Christ Jesus I have begotten you *through the Gospel.* *1 Cor. 4:15.*

436   Neither pray I for these alone, but for them also which shall believe on Me *through their word. John 17:20.*

437   Being *born again*, not of corruptible seed, but of incorruptible, *by the Word of God*, which liveth and abideth forever. *1 Peter 1:23.*

438   According to His mercy He saved us by the *washing of regeneration and renewing of the Holy Ghost. Titus 3:5.* (Baptism.)

169. What else has the Holy Ghost wrought in you by the Gospel?

The Holy Ghost has *sanctified me in the true faith,* that is, He has by faith in Christ *renewed my heart,* so that I can now overcome sin and *do good works.* (Sanctification in the narrower sense.)

439   This is the will of God, even your *sanctification.* *1 Thess. 4:3.*

440   If any man be *in Christ,* he is a *new creature.* *2 Cor. 5:17.*

441   Create in me *a clean heart,* O God, and renew a right spirit within me. *Ps. 51:10.*

442   We are His workmanship, created in Christ Jesus *unto good works,* which God hath before ordained that we should walk in them. *Eph. 2:10.*

170. What is a good work in the sight of God?

In the sight of God a good work is everything that a child of God *does, speaks,* or *thinks in faith* according to the *Ten Commandments,* for the *glory of God,* for the *benefit of his neighbor.*

443   *Without faith* it is impossible to please Him [God]. *Heb. 11:6.*

444   He that *abideth in Me* and I in him, the same bringeth forth much fruit; for *without Me* ye can do nothing. *John 15:5.*

445   In *vain* they do worship Me, teaching for doctrines the *commandments of men.* *Matt. 15:9.*

446   If ye love Me, keep *My commandments.* *John 14:15.*

447   Whether therefore ye eat or drink, or whatsoever ye do, do all to the *glory of God.* *1 Cor. 10:31.*

448   By love *serve one another.* Gal. 5:13.

Bible Narratives: The widow's mite. *Mark 12:41-44.* — The precious ointment poured on Jesus' head. *Mark 14:3-9.* — Mary and Martha. *Luke 10:38-42.*

171. What has the Holy Ghost lastly wrought in you by the Gospel?

The Holy Ghost has, by the Gospel, *kept* me in the true faith.

449   [Ye] are *kept* by the power of God through faith unto salvation. *1 Peter 1:5.*

450   He which hath begun a good work in you *will perform it* until the Day of Jesus Christ. *Phil. 1:6.*

451   The Word of God . . . effectually worketh also in you that believe. *1 Thess. 2:13.*

172. In whom does the Holy Ghost likewise work all that He has wrought in you?

The Holy Ghost calls, gathers, enlightens, and sanctifies the *whole Christian Church* on earth and keeps it with Jesus Christ in the one true faith.

173. Does the Holy Ghost desire to work all this in everyone who hears the Gospel?

The Holy Ghost desires to bring *all men* to salvation by the Gospel.

452   As I live, saith the Lord God, I have *no pleasure* in the death of the wicked; but that the *wicked turn* from his way and live. *Ezek. 33:11.*

453   The Lord . . . is *not willing that any should perish,* but that *all* should come to repentance. *2 Peter 3:9.*

454   [God] will have *all men to be saved* and to come unto the knowledge of the truth. *1 Tim. 2:4.*

174. Why, then, are not all men saved?

Because many in unbelief stubbornly resist the Word and the Spirit of God and are thus *lost by their own fault.*

455   O Jerusalem, Jerusalem, thou that killest the prophets and stonest them which are sent unto thee, how often *would I* have gathered thy children together, even as a hen gathereth her chickens under her wings, and *ye would not!* Matt. 23:37.

456   O Israel, *thou* hast *destroyed thyself;* but *in Me* is thine help. *Hos. 13:9.*

457   Ye *stiff-necked* and uncircumcised in heart and ears, ye do always *resist the Holy Ghost;* as your fathers did, so do ye. *Acts 7:51*

Bible Narratives: The guests refused to accept the invitation. *Luke 14:16-24.* — The invited guests refused to come. *Matt. 22:1-10.*

The Ark of the
Church

II. THE HOLY CHRISTIAN CHURCH, OR THE COMMUNION OF SAINTS

175. What is the holy Christian Church?

The holy Christian Church is the communion of saints, that is, the *whole number of believers in Christ;* for all believers, and *only* believers, are members of this Church. (The invisible Church.)

458   Ye are no more strangers and foreigners, but *fellow citizens* with the saints and of the *household* of God; and

are built upon the foundation of the Apostles and Prophets,
Jesus Christ Himself being the chief Cornerstone; in whom
all the *building*, fitly framed together, groweth unto an holy
temple in the Lord; in whom ye also are builded together
for an habitation of God through the Spirit. *Eph. 2:19-22.*

459 As we have many members in one body . . . so we,
being many, are *one body in Christ. Rom. 12:4, 5.*

460 If any man have *not the Spirit* of Christ, he is *none
of His. Rom. 8:9.*

176. Why do you say, "I believe" in the Church?

I say, I *believe* in the Church —

A. Because the Church is *invisible*, since no
man can look into another's heart and see whether
he believes;

461 The kingdom of God cometh *not with observation;*
neither shall they say, Lo, here! or, Lo, there! For, behold,
the kingdom of God is within you. Luke 17:20, 21.

462 The foundation of God standeth sure, having this seal,
The *Lord knoweth* them that are His. *2 Tim. 2:19.*

B. Because we are nevertheless *assured* by
the Scriptures that the Holy Ghost *at all times
gathers and preserves* a congregation of believers.

463 Thou art Peter, and upon this rock I will build My
Church; and the gates of hell *shall not prevail* against it.
Matt. 16:18.

Bible Narrative: The seven thousand in Israel. *1 Kings
19:8-18.*

The City on the Rock

177. Why do you say, I believe in "the" Church?

I say, I believe in *the* Church because there is *only one* Church; for all believers are a *communion* of saints, or one spiritual body, whose one and only Head is Christ.

464   [Endeavor] to keep the unity of the Spirit in the bond of peace. There is *one body* and *one Spirit*, even as ye are called in one hope of your calling; *one Lord, one faith, one Baptism*, one God and Father of all, who is above all and through all and in you all. *Eph. 4:3-6.*

465   As we have many members in one body . . . so we, being *many*, are *one body in Christ*. *Rom. 12:4, 5.*

466   [Christ] is the *Head* of the body, the Church. *Col. 1:18.*

178. Why is the Church called "holy"?

The Church is called *holy* because it is the communion of *saints*, who are made *holy by faith in Christ* and who *serve God with holy works*.

467   Christ also loved the Church and gave Himself for it that He might *sanctify and cleanse it* with the washing of water by the word that He might present it to Himself a *glorious Church*, not having spot or wrinkle or any such thing, but that it should be *holy and without blemish*. *Eph. 5:25-27.*

468   Ye also, as lively stones, are built up a spiritual house, an *holy* priesthood, to offer up *spiritual sacrifices*, acceptable to God by Jesus Christ. *1 Peter 2:5.*

179. Why is the Church called the "Christian" Church?

It is called the *Christian* Church because it is *built upon Christ*, its one and only Foundation.

NOTE. — When the word "catholic" is used (see the Athanasian Creed, p. 53, in the *Lutheran Hymnal*), it means *universal* or *general*, because the Church is found wherever the Gospel is preached.

469   Other *foundation* can no man lay than that is laid, which is *Jesus Christ. 1 Cor. 3:11.*

NOTE. — Eph. 2:19-22.   See 458.

180. Where is this holy Christian Church to be found?

This holy Christian Church is to be found *wherever the Gospel is in use;* for according to God's promise His Word shall not be preached in vain.

470   As the rain cometh down, and the snow, from heaven, and returneth not thither, but watereth the earth and maketh it bring forth and bud that it may give seed to the sower and bread to the eater, so shall *My Word* be that goeth forth out of My mouth; it shall *not return unto Me void,* but it shall *accomplish that which I please,* and it shall *prosper* in the thing whereto I sent it. *Is. 55:10, 11.*

Triumph of the
Gospel

181. In which other senses is the word "church" used?

The word "church" is also used to denote —

A. The visible Church of God.

B. A denomination.

C. A local congregation.

D. A house of worship.

182. What is the visible Church?

The visible Church is the whole number of those who *use the Word of God and profess the Christian faith,* but among whom, besides the true Christians, there are also hypocrites.

The Dragnet

Bible Narratives: The net that gathered of every kind. *Matt. 13:47, 48.* — The man without a wedding garment. *Matt. 22:11, 12.* — Ananias and Sapphira. *Acts 5:1-11.*

183. What is a religious denomination?

A religious denomination is a church organization with a *distinct name and distinctive doctrines.*

184. Which denomination is the true visible Church?

That denomination is the true visible Church which *has, teaches,* and *confesses* the *entire* doctrine of the Word of God and administers the Sacraments *according to Christ's institution.*

471   Teaching them to observe *all things* whatsoever I have commanded you. *Matt. 28:20.*

472   He that hath My Word, let him *speak My Word faithfully. Jer. 23:28.*

473   In vain they do worship Me, teaching for doctrines the commandments of men. *Matt. 15:9.*

185. What is a local church, or congregation?

A local church, or congregation, is a group of professing Christians who *regularly assemble for worship* at one place.

NOTE. — 1 Cor. 1:2 Paul writes to "the church which is at Corinth"; Gal. 1:2 he writes to "the churches of Galatia"; 1 Thess. 1:1 he writes to "the church of the Thessalonians"; Rev. 1-3 John writes to the seven churches of Asia Minor.

186. When do we use the doctrine of the Church properly?

We use the doctrine of the Church properly —

A. **When we take heed to** *be and remain members of the invisible Church* **by sincere faith in the Redeemer;**

✗ 474   Examine yourselves whether ye *be in the faith;* prove your own selves. *2 Cor. 13:5.*

✗ 475   If ye *continue in My Word,* then are ye *My disciples indeed;* and ye shall know the truth, and the truth shall make you free. *John 8:31, 32.*

B. **When we** *adhere to the Church* **which teaches the Word of God in** *all its purity;*

NOTE. — See 475.

✗ 476   They continued *steadfastly in the Apostles' doctrine.* Acts 2:42.

C. **When we do all in our power to** *maintain promote,* **and** *extend* **this Church by** *prayer, personal service,* **and** *financial support;*

NOTE. — See "What the Hearers Owe to Their Pastors," page 25. (The Christian as a steward.)

477   They that were *scattered abroad went everywhere, preaching the Word.* Acts 8:4.

478   Go ye, therefore, and *teach all nations,* baptizing them in the name of the Father and of the Son and of the Holy Ghost. *Matt. 28:19.*

479 So hath the Lord ordained that they which preach the Gospel should *live of the Gospel. 1 Cor. 9:14.*

Bible Narratives: The early Christians prayed for the spreading of the Gospel. *Acts 4:23-30.* — They also contributed to the support of the ministry. *Phil. 4:16-19.*

D. When we *avoid all false churches* and all *other organizations* that profess a *religion that is false.*

480 *Beware of false prophets,* which come to you in sheep's clothing; but inwardly they are ravening wolves. *Matt. 7:15.*

481 Beloved, believe not every spirit, but *try the spirits whether they are of God;* because *many false prophets* are gone out into the world. *1 John 4:1.*

482 Now, I beseech you, brethren, mark them which *cause divisions and offenses contrary to the doctrine* which ye have learned; and *avoid them. Rom. 16:17.*

483 Be ye not unequally yoked together with unbelievers. For what fellowship hath righteousness with unrighteousness? And what communion hath light with darkness? And what concord hath Christ with Belial? Or what part hath he that believeth with an infidel? And what agreement hath the temple of God with idols? For ye are the temple of the living God, as God hath said, I will dwell in them and walk in them; and I will be their God, and they shall be My people. Wherefore *come out from among them,* and be ye separate, saith the Lord, and touch not the unclean thing; and I will receive you and will be a Father unto you, and ye shall be My sons and daughters, saith the Lord Almighty. *2 Cor. 6:14-18.*

Wheat and Tares

III. THE FORGIVENESS OF SINS

187. Why do you say, I believe in the forgiveness of sins?

The Bible assures me that *God daily and richly forgives* all sins to me and all believers.

484   Bless the Lord, O my soul, and forget not all His benefits; who *forgiveth all thine iniquities;* who healeth all thy diseases. *Ps. 103:2, 3.*

485   If Thou, Lord, shouldest mark iniquities, O Lord, who shall stand? But there *is forgiveness with Thee* that Thou mayest be feared. *Ps. 130:3, 4.*

188. How does God forgive your sins?

God no longer *charges,* or imputes, *my sins to me,* but *declares me righteous.* (Justification.)

486   God was in Christ, reconciling the world unto Himself, *not imputing* their trespasses unto them. *2 Cor. 5:19.*

487   He hath made Him to be sin for us who knew no sin that we might be *made the righteousness* of God in Him. *2 Cor. 5:21.*

488   Who shall *lay* anything *to the charge* of God's elect? It is God that *justifieth.* *Rom. 8:33.*

489   To him that worketh not, but believeth on Him that *justifieth the ungodly,* his faith is counted for righteousness. *Rom. 4:5.*

Bible Narrative: The king forgave the servant all his debts. *Matt. 18:23-35.*

189. What induces God to forgive your sins?

God forgives my sins, not because of any merit or worthiness in me, but because of *His grace, for Christ's sake.*

490 There is no difference; for all have sinned and come short of the glory of God, being *justified freely by His grace,* through the redemption that is *in Christ Jesus. Rom. 3:22-24.*

491 In whom [Christ] we have redemption through His blood, the *forgiveness of sins,* according to the riches of *His grace. Eph. 1:7.*

Bible Narrative: The publican in the Temple. *Luke 18:9-14.*

190. For whom has this forgiveness been obtained?

Forgiveness of sins has been obtained *for all,* because *Christ* has fully atoned *for the sins of all mankind.*

492 He is the Propitiation for our sins, and *not for ours only,* but also for the sins of *the whole world. 1 John 2:2.*

493 God was in Christ, reconciling *the world* unto Himself, not imputing their trespasses unto them. *2 Cor. 5:19.*

191. Where does God offer you the forgiveness of sins?

God offers me the forgiveness of sins *in the Gospel.*

494 Repentance and *remission of sins* should be *preached* in His name among all nations. *Luke 24:47.*

495 [He] hath committed unto us *the Word of Reconciliation. 2 Cor. 5:19.*

192. How do you accept this forgiveness of sins?

I accept this forgiveness *by believing* the Gospel.

496 A man is justified *by faith,* without the deeds of the Law. *Rom. 3:28.*

497   [Abram] *believed* in the Lord; and He counted it to him for righteousness. *Gen. 15:6.*

NOTE. — See 489.

193. Why can and should every believer be certain of the forgiveness of his sins and of his salvation?

Every believer can and should be certain of the forgiveness of his sins and of his salvation, because *God's promise is sure.*

498   I *know* whom I have believed and am *persuaded* that He is able to keep that which I have committed unto Him against that Day. *2 Tim. 1:12.*

499   *I am persuaded* that neither death nor life nor angels nor principalities nor powers nor things present nor things to come nor height nor depth nor any other creature shall be able to separate us from the love of God, which is in Christ Jesus, our Lord. *Rom. 8:38, 39.*

194. Why must we ever firmly maintain the doctrine of justification by grace, for Christ's sake, through faith?

We must ever firmly maintain this doctrine —

A. Because it is the *chief doctrine* of the Christian religion;

500   To Him give *all the Prophets* witness that through His name *whosoever believeth in Him* shall receive remission of sins. *Acts 10:43.*

501   Neither is there salvation *in any other;* for there is *none other name* under heaven given among men whereby we must be saved. *Acts 4:12.*

B. Because it *distinguishes the Christian religion from false religions,* all of which teach salvation by works;

502 Christ is become of no effect unto you whosoever of *you are justified by the Law;* ye are fallen from grace. For we through the Spirit wait for the *hope of righteousness by faith. Gal. 5:4, 5.*

NOTE. — See Micah 7:18-20.

C. Because this doctrine gives *enduring comfort* to penitent sinners;

503 Sirs, what must I do to be saved? And they said, Believe on the Lord Jesus Christ, and thou shalt be saved and thy house. . . . He set meat before them *and rejoiced,* believing in God with all his house. *Acts 16:30, 31, 34.*

504 Son, be of *good cheer;* thy sins be forgiven thee. *Matt. 9:2.*

D. Because this doctrine gives *all glory to God.*

505 Unto Him that loved us and *washed us from our sins* in His own blood and hath made us kings and priests unto God and His Father; *to Him be glory* and dominion forever and ever. Amen. *Rev. 1:5, 6.*

IV. THE RESURRECTION OF THE BODY

195. What do the Scriptures teach of the resurrection of the body?

The Scriptures teach that at the Last Day God *will raise up me and all the dead,* so that our bodies, the *same* bodies that have died, shall be *made alive.*

506 The hour is coming in the which *all that are in the graves* shall hear His voice and shall come forth. *John 5: 28, 29.*

507   I know that my Redeemer liveth and that He shall stand
at the Latter Day upon the earth; and though after my skin
worms destroy *this body*, yet *in my flesh* shall I see God;
whom I shall see for *myself* and *mine eyes shall behold*, and
not another. *Job 19:25-27*.

196. What difference will there be in the resurrection of the dead?

A. The *believers* will rise with glorified
bodies to *everlasting life* in heaven.

508   [Christ] shall change our vile body that it may be
fashioned *like unto His glorious body*. *Phil. 3:21*.

509   We shall not all sleep, but we shall all be *changed*, in
a moment, in the twinkling of an eye, at the last trump;
for the trumpet shall sound, and the dead shall be raised
incorruptible, and we shall be *changed*. *1 Cor. 15:51, 52*.

510   [They] shall come forth; they that have done good,
unto *the resurrection of life;* and they that have done evil,
unto the resurrection of damnation. *John 5:29*.

511   Though after my skin worms destroy this body, yet *in
my flesh shall I see God;* whom I shall see for myself, and
mine eyes shall behold, and not another. *Job 19:26, 27*.

B. The *unbelievers* will rise to *eternal death*,
that is, to everlasting shame, contempt, and torment in hell.

512   In hell he lifted up his eyes, being *in torments*, and
seeth Abraham afar off and Lazarus in his bosom. And he
cried and said, Father Abraham, have mercy on me and send
Lazarus that he may dip the tip of his finger in water and cool
my tongue; for I am *tormented* in this flame. *Luke 16:23, 24*.
NOTE. — See 510.

513   Fear not them which kill the body, but are not able to
kill the soul; but rather fear Him which is able to destroy
both *soul and body in hell*. *Matt. 10:28*.

⁵¹⁴ Their worm shall *not die*, neither shall their fire be *quenched;* and they shall be an *abhorring* unto all flesh. *Is. 66:24.*

⁵¹⁵ Enter ye in at the strait gate; for wide is the gate, and broad is the way, that leadeth to *destruction;* and many there be which go in thereat. *Matt. 7:13.*

Bible Narrative: The rich man and Lazarus. Two places only. *Luke 16:19-31.* (Degrees of punishment. Luke 12: 47, 48.)

V. THE LIFE EVERLASTING

197. What do the Scriptures teach of eternal life?

The Scriptures teach —

A. That at the time of death the *soul* of the believer is at once received into the presence of Christ;

⁵¹⁶ [I have] a desire to depart and to *be with Christ,* which is far better. *Phil. 1:23.*

⁵¹⁷ Verily I say unto thee, *Today* shalt thou be *with Me* in Paradise. *Luke 23:43.*

⁵¹⁸ *Blessed* are the dead which die in the Lord *from hence-forth;* yea, saith the Spirit, that they may rest from their labors; and their works do follow them. *Rev. 14:13.*

B. That at the Last Day the believer will live with Christ, according to *body and soul,* in eternal joy and glory.

⁵¹⁹ Beloved, now are we the sons of God, and it doth not yet appear what we shall be; but we know that, *when He shall appear,* we shall be like Him; for we shall *see Him* as He is. *1 John 3:2.*

⁵²⁰ In Thy presence is *fullness of joy;* at Thy right hand there are *pleasures forevermore. Ps. 16:11.*

521   Father, I will that they also whom Thou hast given Me *be with Me* where I am, that they may *behold My glory* which Thou hast given Me. *John 17:24.*

522   I reckon that the sufferings of this present time are not worthy to be compared with the *glory* which shall be revealed in us. *Rom. 8:18.*

NOTE. — See Dan. 12:3; Luke 19:16-19; 2 Cor. 9:6. Degrees of eternal glory.

198. To whom will God give eternal life?

God will give eternal life *to me and all believers,* but to believers only.

523   God so loved the world that He gave His only-begotten Son, that *whosoever believeth in Him* should not perish, but have everlasting life. *John 3:16.*

524   He that shall *endure unto the end,* the same shall be saved. *Matt. 24:13.*

525   He that believeth on the Son hath everlasting life; and he that *believeth not* the Son *shall not see life*, but the wrath of God abideth on him. *John 3:36.*

199. Are you sure that you will enter eternal life?

I firmly believe that, as God has in time called me by the Gospel, enlightened, sanctified, and kept me in the true faith, even so He has *from eternity chosen me unto the adoption of children* and *unto life everlasting,* and *no man shall pluck me out of His hand.* (Election of grace; predestination.)

526   Blessed be the God and Father of our Lord Jesus Christ, who *hath blessed us with all spiritual blessings* in heavenly places in Christ; according as He hath chosen us in Him before the foundation of the world, that we should be holy and without blame before Him in love, having *predestinated*

us unto the adoption of children by Jesus Christ to Himself according to the good pleasure of His will, to the praise of the glory of His grace, wherein He hath made us accepted in the Beloved. *Eph. 1:3-6.*

527   We know that all things work together for good to them that love God, to them who are the called according to His purpose.   For whom He did foreknow He also did predestinate to be conformed to the image of His Son that He might be the First-born among many brethren.   Moreover, *whom He did predestinate,* them He also *called;* and whom He called, them He also *justified;* and whom He justified, them He also *glorified. Rom. 8:28-30.*

528   My sheep hear My voice, and I know them, and they follow Me; and I *give unto them eternal life;* and they shall never perish, neither shall any man *pluck them out of My hand. John 10:27, 28.*

200. Why do you close this article with the words "This is most certainly true"?

Because all that I confess in this article is plainly taught in the Bible; therefore I firmly believe it.

The Incense
of Prayer

PART III

The Lord's Prayer

201. What is prayer?

Prayer is an act of worship wherein we bring our *petitions* before God with our *hearts and lips* and offer up *praise* and *thanksgiving* to Him.

529 Let the *words of my mouth* and the *meditation of my heart* be acceptable in Thy sight, O Lord, my Strength and my Redeemer. *Ps. 19:14.*

530 When ye pray, use *not vain repetitions,* as the heathen do; for they think that they shall be heard for *their much speaking.* *Matt. 6:7.*

531 Lord, Thou hast heard the *desire* of the humble. *Ps. 10:17.*

532 And it shall come to pass that, *before they call,* I will answer; and *while they are yet speaking,* I will hear. *Is. 65:24.*

NOTE. — See Ps. 103:1; Ps. 118:1; Ps. 95; Ps. 96.

202. To whom should we pray?

We should pray only to the *true God,* Father, Son, and Holy Ghost, since to Him alone such honor is due and He alone is able and willing to hear and grant our prayer.

533 Thou shalt worship *the Lord, thy God,* and *Him only* shalt thou serve. *Matt. 4:10.*

534 O Thou that *hearest prayer,* unto Thee shall all flesh come. *Ps. 65:2.*

535 Doubtless Thou art our Father, though *Abraham be ignorant of us,* and *Israel acknowledge us not;* Thou, O Lord, art our Father, our Redeemer; Thy name is from everlasting. *Is. 63:16.* (Saints cannot hear prayer.)

203. What should move us to pray?

God's *command* and *promise,* our *own* and *our neighbor's need,* and *gratitude* for blessings received should move us to pray.

536 *Ask,* and it shall be *given* you; *seek,* and ye shall *find; knock,* and it shall be *opened* unto you. For everyone that asketh, receiveth; and he that seeketh, findeth; and to him that knocketh it shall be opened. *Matt. 7:7, 8.*

537 Call upon Me in the *day of trouble;* I will *deliver thee,* and thou shalt *glorify Me. Ps. 50:15.*

Bible Narratives: The leper was induced to pray by his own need. *Luke 5:12, 13.* — The centurion was induced to pray by the need of his servant. *Matt. 8:5-13.* — The healed leper's gratitude moved him to thank Christ. *Luke 17:15, 16.*

204. What should we ask of God in our prayers?

We should ask for *everything* that tends to the *glory of God* and to *our own* and *our neighbor's welfare,* both spiritual and bodily blessings.

538 Be careful for nothing; but *in everything* by prayer and supplication, with thanksgiving, let your requests be made known unto God. *Phil. 4:6.*

539 *What things soever ye desire,* when ye pray, believe that ye receive them, and ye shall have them. *Mark 11:24.*

NOTE. — See 1 Cor. 10:31.

205. What distinction should we make in our prayers?

When praying for *spiritual blessings*, necessary for our salvation, we should ask unconditionally; when praying for *other gifts*, we should ask that God grant them to us if it be His will.

540 If ye, then, being evil, know how to give good gifts unto your children, how much more shall your heavenly Father *give the Holy Spirit* to them that ask Him! *Luke 11:13.*

541 Father, *if Thou be willing,* remove this cup from Me; nevertheless *not My will,* but *Thine,* be done. *Luke 22:42.*

542 Lord, *if Thou wilt,* Thou canst make me clean. *Matt. 8:2.*

543 This is the confidence that we have in Him, that, if we ask anything *according to His will,* He heareth us. *1 John 5:14.*

206. How should we pray?

We should pray —

A. *In the name of Jesus,* that is, with faith in Him as our Redeemer;

544 Verily, verily, I say unto you, Whatsoever ye shall ask the Father *in My name,* He will give it you. *John 16:23.*

B. *With confidence,* that is, with firm trust that for Jesus' sake our prayer will be answered.

545 All things whatsoever ye shall ask in prayer, *believing,* ye shall receive. *Matt. 21:22.*

207. Does God really answer every proper prayer?

God answers every proper prayer, but *in His own way* and *at His own time.*

546 For this thing I besought the Lord thrice that it might depart from me. And He said unto me, My grace is sufficient for thee; for My strength is made perfect in weakness. *2 Cor. 12:8, 9.*

547 *Mine hour* is not yet come. *John 2:4.*

548 *For a small moment* have I forsaken thee; but with great mercies *will I gather thee.* In a little wrath I hid My face from thee *for a moment;* but with everlasting kindness *will I have mercy on thee,* saith the Lord, thy Redeemer. *Is. 54:7, 8.*

208. What prayers has God not promised to answer?

God has not promised to answer prayers —

A. Which are not offered in faith and with confidence;

549 Let him ask *in faith,* nothing wavering. For *he that wavereth* is like a wave of the sea driven with the wind and tossed. For *let not that man think that he shall receive* anything of the Lord. *James 1:6, 7.*

B. Which ask for *foolish and hurtful things;*

Bible Narrative: The mother of Zebedee's children. *Matt. 20:20-23.*

C. Which prescribe to God the *time* when He should help *and the manner* in which He should help.

209. Why do Christians sometimes feel that their proper prayers are not answered?

Christians sometimes feel that their proper prayers are not answered because in the hour of trial they *do not at once observe the helping hand of God.*

NOTE. — See Ps. 42:9.

210. For whom should we pray?

We should pray for *ourselves* and for *all other* people, even for our enemies; but *not for the souls of the dead.*

550   I exhort, therefore, that, first of all, supplications, prayers, intercessions, and giving of thanks be made *for all men. 1 Tim. 2:1.*

551   Pray for them which *despitefully use you and persecute you. Matt. 5:44.*

552   It is appointed unto men once to *die,* but *after this the Judgment. Heb. 9:27.*

Bible Narratives: The publican prayed for himself. *Luke 18:13.* — Abraham prayed for Sodom. *Gen. 18:23-32.* — The Syrophoenician woman prayed for her daughter. *Matt. 15: 22-28.* — Jesus prayed for His enemies. *Luke 23:34.* — Stephen prayed for his enemies. *Acts 7:60.*

211. Where should we pray?

We should pray *everywhere,* especially in *private,* that is, when we are alone, in the family circle, and in *public* worship.

553   I will therefore that men pray *everywhere,* lifting up holy hands, without wrath and doubting. *1 Tim. 2:8.*

554   Thou, when thou prayest, enter into *thy closet;* and when thou hast shut thy door, pray to thy Father, which is *in secret;* and thy Father, which seeth in secret, shall reward thee openly. *Matt. 6:6.*

555   In the *congregations* will I bless the Lord. *Ps. 26:12.*

212. When should we pray?

We should pray *at all times*, especially *in time of trouble*.

556   Pray *without ceasing. 1 Thess. 5:17.*

557   Call upon Me in the *day of trouble.* I will deliver thee, and thou shalt glorify Me. *Ps. 50:15.*

NOTE. — See Ps. 55:16, 17.

Bible Narrative: Daniel prayed three times a day. *Dan. 6:10.*

NOTE. — See Morning and Evening Prayers, pages 22 and 23.

213. Which is the most excellent of all prayers?

The most excellent of all prayers is *the Lord's Prayer,* taught by the Lord Jesus Himself in the words:

Our Father who art in heaven. Hallowed be Thy name. Thy kingdom come. Thy will be done on earth as it is in heaven. Give us this day our daily bread. And forgive us our trespasses, as we forgive those who trespass against us. And lead us not into temptation, but deliver us from evil. For Thine is the kingdom and the power and the glory forever and ever. Amen. *(Matt. 6:9-13; Luke 11:2-4.)*

214. How may the Lord's Prayer be divided?

The Lord's Prayer may be divided into the *Introduction,* the *Seven Petitions,* and the *Conclusion.*

THE INTRODUCTION

Our Father who art in heaven.

What does this mean? God would by
these words tenderly invite us to believe
that He is our true Father, and that we
are His true children, so that we may
with all boldness and confidence ask
Him as dear children ask their dear
father.

**215. Why does Jesus in this prayer teach us to
call God "Father"?**

He would by this winning name *encourage*
us to *pray without fear or doubt.*

558   Behold, what manner of love the Father hath bestowed
upon us that we should be called the *sons of God! 1 John 3:1.*

559   Ye have not received the spirit of bondage again to
fear; but ye have received the Spirit of adoption, whereby
we cry, Abba, *Father. Rom. 8:15.*

216. Why do we say "our Father"?

We say *"our* Father" because the *believers*
in Christ throughout the world are the *children
of one Father* and therefore pray *for* and *with*
one another.

560   One God and Father of all, who is above all and
through all and in you all. *Eph. 4:6.*

561   Ye are all the children of God by faith in Christ Jesus.
Gal. 3:26.

217. Why do we say "who art in heaven"?

These words are to remind us that our Father is *Lord over all* and is therefore *able to do far more than we can ask or think*. Eph. 3:20.

218. What do we ask in the seven petitions?

In the first three petitions we ask for spiritual blessings, in the Fourth Petition for material gifts, and in the last three petitions for deliverance from evil.

THE FIRST PETITION

Hallowed be Thy name.

What does this mean? God's name is indeed holy in itself; but we pray in this petition that it may be holy among us also.

How is this done? · [God's name is hallowed] When the Word of God is taught in its truth and purity, and we, as the children of God, also lead a holy life according to it. This grant us, dear Father in heaven. But he that teaches and lives otherwise than God's Word teaches, profanes the name of God among us. From this preserve us, Heavenly Father.

219. How is God's name hallowed?

God's name is hallowed —

A. When the Word of God is *taught in its truth and purity;*

562   Sanctify them through Thy truth; *Thy Word is truth.* John 17:17.

563   He that hath My Word, let him speak My Word *faithfully.* Jer. 23:28.

B. When we, as the children of God, also *lead a holy life* according to the Word of God.

564   Let your light so shine before men that they may see your *good works* and *glorify your Father* which is in heaven. Matt. 5:16.

220. How is God's name profaned?

God's name is profaned —

A. When anyone *teaches otherwise* than God's Word teaches;

565   Her priests have *violated* My Law and have *profaned* Mine holy things. *Ezek. 22:26.*

B. When anyone *lives otherwise* than God's Word teaches.

566   Thou that makest thy boast of the Law, *through breaking* the Law *dishonorest thou God?* For the name of God is *blasphemed among the Gentiles* through you. *Rom. 2:23, 24.*

221. What do we ask in the First Petition?

We ask that God's name be hallowed *among us.*

THE SECOND PETITION
Thy kingdom come.

What does this mean? The kingdom of God comes indeed without our prayer, of itself; but we pray in this petition that it may come unto us also.

How is this done? [The kingdom of God comes to us] When our heavenly Father gives us His Holy Spirit, so that by His grace we believe His holy Word and lead a godly life, here in time and hereafter in eternity.

222. Which kingdom do we mean in the Second Petition?

We mean God's *Kingdom of Grace* and His *Kingdom of Glory,* but not His Kingdom of Power.

223. What do we ask in this petition?

We ask —

A. That God would graciously grant us *true faith* and a *godly life;*

567   The kingdom of God is at hand; repent ye, and believe the Gospel. *Mark 1:15.*

568   As ye have, therefore, received Christ Jesus, the Lord, so *walk* ye in Him. *Col. 2:6.*

B. That He would *extend His Kingdom of Grace* on earth (missions);

569   Pray ye therefore the Lord of the harvest that He will
send forth laborers into His harvest. *Matt. 9:38.*

570   Brethren, pray for us that *the Word of the Lord may
have free course* and be glorified. *2 Thess. 3:1.*

Bible Narrative: Mission prayer. *Acts 4:24-30.*

c. That He would *hasten the coming of His
Kingdom of Glory.*

571   Fear not, little flock; for it is your Father's good
pleasure *to give you the Kingdom. Luke 12:32.*

572   He which testifieth these things saith, Surely, I come
quickly. Amen. Even so, *come, Lord Jesus. Rev. 22:20.*

THE THIRD PETITION

Thy will be done on earth as it is in heaven.

What does this mean? The good and
gracious will of God is done indeed
without our prayer; but we pray in
this petition that it may be done among
us also.

How is this done? [God's good and
gracious will is done among us] When
God breaks and hinders every evil
counsel and will which would not let
us hallow God's name nor let His kingdom come, such as the will of the devil,
the world, and our flesh; but strengthens and preserves us steadfast in His
Word and faith unto our end. This
is His gracious and good will.

---

224. What is the good and gracious will of God?

The good and gracious will, of God is that we *hallow His name* and that *His kingdom come.*

225. What does the good and gracious will of God include?

This good and gracious will of God includes —

A. Everything that God wants *to do for us* according to His promise;

573   [God] will have all men *to be saved* and to come unto the knowledge of the truth. *1 Tim. 2:4.*

B. Everything that God *wants us to do and to avoid* according to His will;

574   This is the will of God, even your sanctification. *1 Thess. 4:3.*

C. Everything that God wants us to *suffer patiently* according to His good pleasure.

575   We must through *much tribulation* enter into the kingdom of God. *Acts 14:22.*

576   Then said Jesus unto His disciples, If any man will come after Me, let him *deny himself and take up his cross* and follow Me. *Matt. 16:24.*

NOTE. — See Heb. 12:6, 11.

226. Whose counsel and will are opposed to the will of God?

The counsel and will of the *devil,* the *world,* and our *flesh* are opposed to the will of God.

577   The *devil*, as a roaring lion, walketh about, seeking whom he may devour. *1 Peter 5:8.*

578   Love not the *world*, neither the things that are in the world. If any man love the world, the love of the Father is not in him. For all that is in the *world*, the lust of the *flesh* and the lust of the eyes and the pride of life, *is not of the Father*, but is of the world. And the world passeth away and the lust thereof; but he that doeth the will of God abideth forever. *1 John 2:15-17.*

579   I know that in me (that is, *in my flesh*) dwelleth no good thing. *Rom. 7:18.*

Bible Narratives: The devil misled man to sin. *Gen. 3:1-7.* — The enemies of Jesus brought about the fall of Peter. *Luke 22:54-62.* — Achan's sinful flesh induced him to steal. *Josh. 7:18-22.*

227. What do we ask of God in the Third Petition?

We ask —

A. That God would *break and hinder* the evil counsel and will of the devil, the world, and our flesh;

580   The God of peace shall *bruise Satan* under your feet shortly. *Rom. 16:20.*

B. That God would *strengthen and preserve* us steadfast in His Word and faith unto our end, so that we may at all times *do His will* as gladly as the angels in heaven;

581   [Ye] are *kept by the power of God* through faith unto salvation. *1 Peter 1:5.*

582   Make me to go in the path of Thy commandments; for therein do I *delight*. *Ps. 119:35.*

c. That God would *in all suffering keep us faithful* to our end.

583   He said unto me, My grace is sufficient for thee; for *My strength is made perfect in weakness. 2 Cor. 12:9.*

NOTE. — See 1 Cor. 10:13.

Bible Narratives: God hindered the evil will of Joseph's brothers and kept him faithful. *Gen. 50:15-21.* — God would not let the devil destroy Job. *Job 1.*

THE FOURTH PETITION

Give us this day our daily bread.

What does this mean? God gives daily bread indeed without our prayer, also to all the wicked; but we pray in this petition that He would lead us to know it, and to receive our daily bread with thanksgiving.

What is meant by daily bread? [Daily bread is] Everything that belongs to the support and wants of the body, such as food, drink, clothing, shoes, house, home, field, cattle, money, goods, a pious spouse, pious children, pious servants, pious and faithful rulers, good government, good weather, peace, health, discipline, honor, good friends, faithful neighbors, and the like.

228. Why does Christ tell us to ask for daily bread, even though God gives it also to those who do not ask for it?

Christ tells us to ask for daily bread in order to teach us that our daily bread is a *gracious gift of God* and that we may *receive it with thanksgiving*.

584   The eyes. of all *wait upon Thee,* and *Thou* givest them their meat in due season. *Thou openest Thine hand* and satisfiest the desire of every living thing. *Ps. 145: 15, 16.*

585   He maketh His sun to rise on the *evil* and on the *good* and sendeth rain on the *just* and on the *unjust. Matt. 5:45.*

586   *Giving thanks always for all things* unto God and the Father in the name of our Lord Jesus Christ. *Eph. 5:20.*

Bible Narratives: Peter's draught of fishes. *Luke 5:1-7.* — Elijah and the widow. *1 Kings 17*

229. Why do we say "our" bread?

We say *"our"* bread because we should ask for that bread only which is honestly ours, and because we should also *pray for our neighbor* and *share* with him when he is in need.

587   If any *would not work, neither should he eat.* For we hear that there are some which walk among you disorderly, working not at all, but are busybodies. Now, them that are

such we command and exhort by our Lord Jesus Christ that
with quietness they *work* and *eat their own* bread. *2 Thess.
3:10-12.*

588   To do good and to *communicate* forget not; for with
such sacrifices God is well pleased. *Heb. 13:16.*

230. Why are we to say "daily" and "this day"?

We are to say "daily" and "this day" because
we should be satisfied with what we *need each
day,* and because it is *foolish* and *sinful* to *worry
about the future.*

589   Two things have I required of Thee; deny me them
not before I die: Remove far from me vanity and lies; give
me *neither poverty nor riches;* feed me with food convenient
for me, lest *I be full* and *deny Thee* and say, Who is the
Lord? or lest *I be poor and steal* and take the name of my
God in vain. *Prov. 30:7-9.*

590   Having *food and raiment,* let us be therewith *content.*
1 Tim. 6:8.

591   Seek ye *first the kingdom of God* and His righteousness;
and all these things shall be *added* unto you. Take therefore
no thought *for the morrow;* for the morrow shall take *thought
for the things of itself.* Sufficient *unto the day* is the evil
thereof. *Matt. 6:33, 34.*

592   It is vain for you to rise up early, to sit up late, to *eat
the bread of sorrows;* for so He giveth His beloved sleep.
Ps. 127:2.

Bible Narrative: The man whose ground had brought forth
plentifully. *Luke 12:15-21.*

THE FIFTH PETITION

And forgive us our trespasses, as we forgive those who trespass against us.

What does this mean? We pray in this petition that our Father in heaven would not look upon our sins, nor on their account deny our prayer; for we are worthy of none of the things for which we pray, neither have we deserved them; but that He would grant them all to us by grace; for we daily sin much and indeed deserve nothing but punishment. So will we also heartily forgive, and readily do good to, those who sin against us.

231. For what do we pray in this petition?

We pray in this petition that our Father in heaven would *not look upon our sins*, but graciously, for Christ's sake, *forgive them.*

593   Who can understand his errors? *Cleanse Thou me from secret faults. Ps. 19:12.*

594   The publican, standing afar off, would not lift up so much as his eyes unto heaven, but smote upon his breast, saying, *God be merciful to me, a sinner. Luke 18:13.*

232. What special reason have we for praying for forgiveness?

We are worthy of none of the things for which we pray, neither have we deserved them;

for we daily sin much and indeed deserve nothing
but punishment.

595   *I am not worthy* of the least of all the mercies and of
all the truth which Thou hast showed unto Thy servant.
Gen. 32:10.

596   Father, *I have sinned* against Heaven and in thy sight
and am *no more worthy* to be called thy son. *Luke 15:21.*

233. What do we gratefully promise for having received forgiveness?

We promise that *we* will also *heartily* forgive, and readily *do good* to, those who sin
against us.

597   Then came Peter to Him and said, Lord, how oft shall
my brother sin against me and *I forgive him?* Till seven
times? Jesus saith unto him, I say not unto thee, Until seven
times; but, Until *seventy times seven. Matt. 18:21, 22.*

Bible Narrative: Joseph forgave his brothers. *Gen. 50:15-21.*

234. Can anyone who will not forgive his neighbor obtain forgiveness from God?

He who will not forgive his neighbor will
not obtain forgiveness from God, but will in this
petition *call down upon himself the anger of God.*

598   When ye stand *praying, forgive* if ye have aught against
any, that your Father also which is in heaven may forgive
you your trespasses. But if ye do not forgive, *neither will
your Father* which is in heaven *forgive* your trespasses.
Mark 11:25, 26.

Bible Narrative: The wicked servant would not forgive his
fellow servant. *Matt. 18:23-35.*

THE SIXTH PETITION

And lead us not into temptation.

What does this mean? God indeed tempts no one; but we pray in this petition that God would guard and keep us, so that the devil, the world, and our flesh may not deceive us nor seduce us into misbelief, despair, and other great shame and vice; and though we be assailed by them, that still we may finally overcome and obtain the victory.

235. In what twofold sense is the word "temptation" used?

The word "temptation" may refer either to an act of testing (trying) or to enticement to evil.

236. In which sense is it said that God tempts man?

God is said to tempt man when He tests, or tries, the faith of His children for the purpose of purifying and strengthening them.

599 [Jesus] saith unto Philip, Whence shall we buy bread that these may eat? And this He said to *prove him;* for He Himself knew what He would do. *John 6:5, 6.*

Bible Narratives: The Lord tempted Abraham in order to test and to strengthen his faith. *Gen. 22:1-19.*—Jesus tempted the Syrophoenician woman in order to test and to strengthen her faith. *Mark 7:25-30.*

237. In which sense is the word "temptation" used in the Sixth Petition?

In this petition the word "temptation" means temptation to evil.

238. In what does temptation to evil consist?

Temptation to evil consists in this, that the devil, the world, and our flesh try to *deceive us* or *seduce us* into misbelief, despair, and other great shame and vice.

600   Let no man say when he is tempted, I am tempted of God; for God cannot be tempted with evil, neither tempteth He any man; but *every man is tempted* when he is drawn away *of his own lust* and enticed. *James 1:13, 14.*

601   Be sober, be vigilant; because your adversary, the *devil,* as a roaring lion, walketh about, *seeking whom he may devour;* whom resist steadfast in the faith. *1 Peter 5:8, 9.*

602   Woe unto the *world* because of *offenses!* For it must needs be that offenses come; but woe to that man by whom the offense cometh! *Matt. 18:7.*

603   My son, if *sinners entice* thee, consent thou not. *Prov. 1:10.*

604   Demas hath forsaken me, having loved this present *world. 2 Tim. 4:10.*

Bible Narratives: The devil tempted Eve to misbelief. *Gen. 3.* — The devil tempted Christ. *Matt. 4:1-11.* — The devil tempted Judas to betray Christ. *John 13:2.* — The devil led Judas into despair. *Matt. 27:4, 5.* — In the high priest's house the world seduced Peter to deny his Savior. *Luke 22:54-60.* — David's flesh tempted him to commit adultery and murder. *2 Sam. 12:9.*

239. What, then, do we ask in the Sixth Petition?

We ask God —

A. To guard and keep us, so that *temptation to evil may not come upon us;*

605   The Lord is faithful, who shall stablish you and *keep you from evil. 2 Thess. 3:3.*

B. *To strengthen and preserve* us when He permits temptation to come, so that in the end we may *overcome and obtain the victory.*

606   God is faithful, who will not suffer you to be tempted above that ye are able, but will, with the temptation, also *make a way to escape* that ye may be *able to bear it. 1 Cor. 10:13.*

607   Take unto you the whole armor of God that ye may be *able to withstand* in the evil day and, having done all, *to stand. Eph. 6:13.*

THE SEVENTH PETITION

But deliver us from evil.

What does this mean? We pray in this petition, as the sum of all, that our Father in heaven would deliver us from every evil of body and soul, property and honor, and finally, when our last hour has come, grant us a blessed end, and graciously take us from this vale of tears to Himself in heaven.

240. What do we ask in the Seventh Petition?

We ask God —

A. To *keep every evil from us;*

608 There shall *no evil* befall thee, neither shall any plague come nigh thy dwelling. *Ps. 91:10.*

B. To *take from us,* or *help us to bear,* and *turn to our own benefit,* the cross with which He afflicts us;

609 We must *through much tribulation* enter into the kingdom of God. *Acts 14:22.*

610 Whom the Lord loveth *He chasteneth,* and *scourgeth every* son whom He receiveth. *Heb. 12:6.*

611 My grace is sufficient for thee; for My strength is made perfect in weakness. *2 Cor. 12:9.*

612 He shall deliver thee in six troubles; yea, in seven there shall *no evil* touch thee. *Job 5:19.*

C. To *deliver* us from *all evil* by a blessed end.

613 The Lord shall deliver me from *every evil* work and will preserve me unto His *heavenly kingdom. 2 Tim. 4:18.*

614 Lord, now lettest Thou Thy servant *depart in peace* according to Thy word; for mine eyes have seen Thy salvation. *Luke 2:29, 30.*

615 [I have] a desire *to depart* and to be *with Christ;* which is *far better. Phil. 1:23.*

THE CONCLUSION

For Thine is the kingdom and the power and the glory forever and ever. Amen.

What is meant by the word "Amen"? That I should be certain that these petitions are acceptable to our Father in heaven, and are heard by Him; for He Himself has commanded us so to pray, and has promised to hear us. Amen, Amen, that is, Yea, yea, it shall be so.

241. What do we state in the Conclusion to the Lord's Prayer?

In the Conclusion we state the reasons for asking all these things of God:

A. He alone is the *King,* from whom we seek help.

B. He alone has the *power* to grant our petitions.

C. He shall have all *glory and praise* for all that He has done for us.

The Sacraments

242. What do we mean by a Sacrament?

By a Sacrament we mean *a sacred act* —

A. Instituted *by God Himself;*

B. In which there are *certain visible means connected with His word;* and

c. By which God *offers, gives,* and *seals* unto us *the forgiveness of sins* which Christ has earned for us.

243. How many such Sacraments are there?

There are *only two* such Sacraments, Holy Baptism and the Lord's Supper.

Baptismal Shell

PART IV

The Sacrament of Holy Baptism

I. THE NATURE OF BAPTISM

What is Baptism?   Baptism is not simple water only, but it is the water comprehended in God's command and connected with God's word.

Which is that word of God?   Christ, our Lord, says in the last chapter of Matthew: Go ye and teach all nations, baptizing them in the name of the Father and of the Son and of the Holy Ghost.

---

244. What is the meaning of the word "baptize"?

"Baptize" means *to apply water* by washing, pouring, sprinkling, or immersing.

616　When they [the Pharisees] come from the market, except they wash [baptize], they eat not. And many other things there be which they have received to hold, as the washing [baptizing] of cups and pots, brazen vessels, and of tables. *Mark 7:4.*

617　Arise and be *baptized* and *wash* away thy sins. *Acts 22:16.*

618　He shall *baptize* you with the Holy Ghost and with fire. *Matt. 3:11.*

NOTE. — Compare Acts 2:16, 17. Note that "baptize" means also "pour out."

245. Why is Baptism not simple water only?

Baptism is not simple water only —

A. Because in Baptism water is used by a special command of God;

B. Because the water is applied in the name of the Father and of the Son and of the Holy Ghost, and is thus connected with God's word.

246. Who instituted Holy Baptism?

God Himself instituted Baptism; for Christ, who is God, commanded His Church to baptize all nations.

619　All power is given unto Me in heaven and in earth. Go ye, therefore, and teach [make disciples of] all nations, *baptizing* them in the name of the Father and of the Son and of the Holy Ghost; teaching them to observe all things whatsoever I have commanded you. And, lo, I am with you alway, even unto the end of the world. *Matt. 28:18-20.*

247. Through whom does the Church administer Baptism?

The Church administers Baptism *through the called ministers* of Christ; but in cases of *emergency* and in the *absence of the pastor,* any Christian should baptize.

NOTE. — For a short form of baptism in cases of necessity see page 212.

620   Let a man so account of us as of the *ministers of Christ* and *stewards of the mysteries of God. 1 Cor. 4:1.*

NOTE. — See The Office of the Keys, Part V, page 181.

248. What do the words "baptize in the name of the Father and of the Son and of the Holy Ghost" imply?

They imply that by Baptism I have been received into *communion with the Triune God.*

249. Who is to be baptized?

All nations, that is, all human beings, *young and old,* are to be baptized.

250. What distinction is to be made in baptizing?

A. Those *who can receive instruction* are to be baptized *after they have been instructed* in the principal doctrines of the Christian religion.

621   They that gladly *received his word* were baptized. *Acts 2:41.*

Bible Narratives: The Ethiopian was instructed before he was baptized. *Acts 8:26-39.* — The jailer was instructed before he was baptized. *Acts 16:25-33.*

B. Little *children* should be baptized when they are brought to Baptism by those *who have authority over them*.

622 Ye *fathers,* provoke not your children to wrath, but bring them up in the nurture and admonition of the Lord. *Eph. 6:4.*

251. How do you prove that infants, too, are to be baptized?

Infants, too, are to be baptized —

A. Because they are *included* in the words "all nations";

623 Go ye therefore and teach *all nations, baptizing them* in the name of the Father and of the Son and of the Holy Ghost. *Matt. 28:19.*

624 Then Peter said unto them, Repent and *be baptized, every one of you,* in the name of Jesus Christ for the remission of sins, and ye shall receive the gift of the Holy Ghost. For the promise is unto you *and to your children. Acts 2:38, 39.*

B. Because Holy Baptism is the *only means* whereby infants, *who, too, must be born again, can ordinarily be regenerated and brought to faith;*

625 They brought young children to Him that He should touch them; and His disciples rebuked those that brought them. But when Jesus saw it, He was much displeased and said unto them, Suffer the little children to come unto Me and forbid them not; for *of such is the kingdom of God.* Verily I say unto you, Whosoever shall not receive the kingdom of God as a little child, he shall not enter therein. *Mark 10:13-15.*

⁶²⁶ Except a man *be born of water and of the Spirit*, he cannot enter into the kingdom of God; that which is *born of the flesh is flesh. John 3:5, 6.*

c. Because infants, too, *can believe.*

⁶²⁷ Whoso shall offend one of these *little ones which believe* in Me, it were better for him that a millstone were hanged about his neck and that he were drowned in the depth of the sea. *Matt. 18:6.*

252. For what purposes has the Church introduced sponsors?

Sponsors are —

A. To *testify* that the children have been *properly baptized;*

⁶²⁸ In the mouth of *two or three witnesses* every word may be established. *Matt. 18:16.*

B. To assist in *caring for the Christian education* and training of their godchildren, especially if these should *lose their parents;*

c. To *pray* for them.

II. THE BLESSINGS OF BAPTISM

What does Baptism give or profit? It works forgiveness of sins, delivers from death and the devil, and gives eternal salvation to all who believe this, as the words and promises of God declare.

Which are such words and promises of God? Christ, our Lord, says in the last chapter of Mark: He that believeth and is baptized shall be saved; but he that believeth not shall be damned.

253. What great things, then, does Baptism give or work?

A. It works *forgiveness of sins;*

629 Repent and *be baptized,* every one of you, in the name of Jesus Christ *for the remission of sins. Acts 2:38.*

630 Arise and be *baptized* and *wash away thy sins. Acts 22:16.*

631 Ye are all the children of God by faith in Christ Jesus. For as many of you as have *been baptized* into Christ have *put on Christ. Gal. 3:26, 27.*

B. It *delivers from death and the devil;*

632 Know ye not that so many of us as were baptized into Jesus Christ were baptized into His death? *Rom. 6:3.*

C. It *gives eternal salvation.*

633 He that believeth and *is baptized* shall be *saved. Mark 16:16.*

634 Baptism doth also now *save us. 1 Peter 3:21.*

254. But has not Christ earned all these blessings for us?

By His suffering and death Christ has indeed earned these blessings for us; Baptism, however, is a *means* by which the Holy Ghost *makes these blessings our own.* (Baptism is a means of grace.)

635   Ye are all the children of God by faith in Christ Jesus. For as many of you as have been baptized into Christ have *put on Christ. Gal. 3:26, 27.*

636   But ye are *washed,* but ye are *sanctified,* but ye are *justified* in the name of the Lord Jesus and *by the Spirit of our God. 1 Cor. 6:11.*

255. To whom does Baptism give all these blessings?

Baptism gives these blessings *to all who believe,* as the words and promises of God declare: "He that *believeth* and is baptized shall be saved; but he that believeth not shall be damned."

256. Can anyone be saved without Baptism?

It is unbelief only that damns; and though saving faith cannot exist in the heart of one who refuses to be baptized, it can exist when for some reason Baptism *cannot* be obtained.

Bible Narrative: The Pharisees and lawyers rejected the counsel of God against themselves when they refused to be baptized by John. *Luke 7:30.*

III. THE POWER OF BAPTISM

How can water do such great things? It is not the water indeed that does them, but the word of God which is in and with the water, and faith, which trusts such word of God in the water. For without the word of God the water is simple water and no Baptism. But with the word of God it is a Baptism, that is, a gracious water of life and a washing of regeneration in the Holy Ghost, as St. Paul says, Titus, chapter third:

[According to His mercy He saved us] By the washing of regeneration and renewing of the Holy Ghost, which He shed on us abundantly through Jesus Christ, our Savior, that, being justified by His grace, we should be made heirs according to the hope of eternal life. This is a faithful saying.

257. How are forgiveness of sins, deliverance from death and the devil, and eternal salvation obtained by Baptism?

The word of God *places these great blessings into Baptism;* and through faith, which trusts this word of promise, *we accept* the forgiveness, life, and salvation offered in Baptism and make these blessings our own.

637   Christ also loved the Church and gave Himself for it that He might sanctify and *cleanse* it with the *washing of water by the word. Eph. 5:25, 26.*

258. Why do the Scriptures call Baptism the washing of regeneration and renewing of the Holy Ghost?

In Baptism the Holy Ghost *works faith* and thus *creates in us new spiritual life*.

IV. THE SIGNIFICANCE OF BAPTIZING WITH WATER

What does such baptizing with water signify? It signifies that the Old Adam in us should, by daily contrition and repentance, be drowned and die with all sins and evil lusts and, again, a new man daily come forth and arise, who shall live before God in righteousness and purity forever.

Where is this written? St. Paul writes, Romans, chapter sixth: We are buried with Christ by Baptism into death, that, like as He was raised up from the dead by the glory of the Father, even so we also should walk in newness of life.

---

259. What is the Old Adam?

The Old Adam is the *sinful nature,* which has come upon us *by the fall of Adam* and is *ours by birth*.

638 Put off concerning the former conversation the old man, which is *corrupt* according to the deceitful lusts. *Eph. 4:22.*

260. How is this Old Adam to be drowned in us?

The Old Adam is to be drowned in us by daily *contrition* (sorrow for sins) and *repentance* (faith), by which we also *resist* the evil desires and *suppress* them.

639 They that are Christ's have *crucified the flesh* with the affections and lusts. *Gal. 5:24.*

261. What is the new man?

The new man is the *new spiritual life*, created in us by the washing of regeneration.

640 If any man be *in Christ*, he is a *new creature.* *2 Cor. 5:17.*

262. How does this new man come forth and arise?

The new man comes forth and arises as we daily overcome sin and live in true godliness.

641 Put on the new man, which after God is created in *righteousness* and *true holiness. Eph. 4:24.*

263. How does baptizing with water signify the daily drowning of the old man and the coming forth of the new man?

By Baptism we are made partakers of Christ. Now we who are baptized should daily repent of all sins, shun everything that is evil, and walk in newness of life.

264. Whom do we therefore renounce at our baptism?

At our baptism we renounce *the devil* and *all his works* and *all his ways*.

265. What promise, or vow, do we make at our baptism?

At our baptism we promise, or vow, *to serve the Triune God*, and *Him only*.

266. When should we renew our baptismal vow?

We should renew our baptismal vow *daily*.

PART V

The Office of the Keys and Confession

What is the Office of the Keys? It is the peculiar church power which Christ has given to His Church on earth to forgive the sins of penitent sinners, but to retain the sins of the impenitent as long as they do not repent.

Where is this written? Thus writes the holy Evangelist John, chapter twentieth: The Lord Jesus breathed on His disciples and saith unto them, Receive ye the Holy Ghost. Whosoever sins ye remit, they are remitted unto them; and whosoever sins ye retain, they are retained.

267. What is the power, or authority, of the Office of the Keys?

The Office of the Keys is the power, or authority, *to preach the Word of God, to admin-*

ister the Sacraments, and especially the power *to forgive and to retain sins.*

642   Ye are a chosen generation, a royal priesthood, an holy nation, a peculiar people; that *ye should show forth the praises of Him* who hath called you out of darkness into His marvelous light. *1 Peter 2:9.*

643   He said unto them, Go ye into all the world, and *preach the Gospel* to every creature. *Mark 16:15.*

644   Jesus came and spake unto them, saying, All power is given unto Me in heaven and in earth. Go ye therefore and teach all nations, baptizing them in the name of the Father and of the Son and of the Holy Ghost; *teaching them* to observe all things whatsoever I have commanded you. And, lo, I am with you alway, even unto the end of the world. *Matt. 28:18-20.*

645   [Christ] breathed on them and saith unto them, Receive ye the Holy Ghost: Whosoever *sins ye remit,* they are remitted unto them; and whosoever *sins ye retain,* they are retained. *John 20:22, 23.*

646   Verily I say unto you, Whatsoever *ye shall bind* on earth shall be bound in heaven; and whatsoever *ye shall loose* on earth shall be loosed in heaven. *Matt. 18:18.*

268. Why is this power called the Office of the Keys?

This power is called the Office of the Keys because it *opens heaven* by forgiving sins, or *closes heaven* by retaining sins.

647   I will give unto thee the *keys of the kingdom of heaven.* *Matt. 16:19.*

269. Why is it called the peculiar church power?

It is called the peculiar church power because it is a power given *only to the Church.*

270. To whom, then, has Christ given this power?

Christ has given this power to His *Church on earth;* especially, to *every local congregation.*

648   Whatsoever *thou* shalt bind on earth shall be bound in heaven; and whatsoever *thou* shalt loose on earth shall be loosed in heaven. *Matt. 16:19.* (To Peter as the spokesman of all disciples.)

649   [Christ] breathed on them and saith unto them, *Receive ye the Holy Ghost.* Whosesoever sins *ye* remit, they are remitted unto them; and whosesoever sins *ye* retain, they are retained. *John 20:22, 23.* (All disciples.)

650   *Ye* are a chosen generation, a *royal priesthood,* an holy nation, a peculiar people; that *ye* should show forth the praises of Him who hath called you out of darkness into His marvelous light. *1 Peter 2:9.* (All Christians.)

651   If he shall neglect to hear them, tell it unto *the church;* but if he neglect to hear *the church,* let him be unto thee as an heathen man and a publican. Verily *I say unto you,* Whatsoever *ye shall bind on earth* shall be bound in heaven; and whatsoever *ye shall loose* on earth shall be loosed in heaven. . . . For where *two or three* are gathered together in My name, there am I in the midst of them. *Matt. 18: 17, 18, 20.* (The local congregation.)

NOTE. — See also texts under Question 267.

271. Whose sins are to be remitted?

The sins of the *penitent* sinners are to be remitted.

652   *Repent* ye, therefore, and be *converted,* that your sins may be *blotted out. Acts 3:19.*

John the Baptist Preacher of Repentance

272. Who are penitent sinners?

Penitent sinners are sinners who *feel sorry for their sins* (contrition) and *believe in the Lord Jesus Christ as their Savior* (faith).

653   The sacrifices of God are a *broken spirit;* a broken
and a *contrite heart,* O God, Thou wilt not despise.
Ps. 51:17.

654   *Believe on the Lord Jesus Christ,* and thou shalt be
saved. *Acts 16:31.*

Bible Narratives: David. See *Psalms 6, 32, 51, 130.* — The
Publican. *Luke 18:13.* — The Prodigal Son. *Luke 15:11-24.* —
Peter. *Matt. 26:75.*

273. What is the necessary fruit of true repentance?

The necessary fruit of true repentance is
a truly Christian life.

655   Bring forth, therefore, *fruits meet for repentance.*
Matt. 3:8.
NOTE. — See Gal. 5:22-24.

274. Whose sins are to be retained?

The sins *of the impenitent* sinners, that is, of
those who are *not* sorry *for their sins* and *do not
believe in Jesus Christ,* are to be retained as long
as they do not repent.

THE OFFICE OF THE MINISTRY

*What do you believe according to these
words (John 20:22, 23)?* I believe that,
when the called ministers of Christ deal
with us by His divine command, especially when they exclude manifest and
impenitent sinners from the Christian

congregation, and, again, when they absolve those who repent of their sins and are willing to amend, this is as valid and certain, in heaven also, as if Christ, our dear Lord, dealt with us Himself.

275. How does the local congregation publicly administer the Office of the Keys?

According to God's will the Christian congregation chooses and calls men as ministers, who in the name of Christ and in the name of the congregation publicly perform the functions of the Office of the Keys. (The pastoral office a divine institution, Acts 20:28; Eph. 4:10-12.)

656 Let a man so account of us as of the *ministers of Christ* and *stewards of the mysteries of God. 1 Cor. 4:1.*

657 Take heed therefore unto yourselves, and to all the flock, over the which the *Holy Ghost* hath made you overseers. *Acts 20:28.*

658 If I forgave anything, to whom I forgave it, *for your sakes* forgave I it *in the person of Christ. 2 Cor. 2:10.*

659 Let the woman learn in silence with all subjection. But I suffer not a woman to teach, nor to usurp authority over the man, but to be in silence. *1 Tim. 2:11, 12.*

276. How do the called ministers of Christ deal with us by His divine command?

The called ministers of Christ preach the Word of God, administer the Sacraments, and through these means of grace offer and convey the forgiveness of sins. This is *as valid,* in heaven also, *as if Christ,* our dear Lord, *dealt with us Himself.*

CHURCH DISCIPLINE AND EXCOMMUNICATION

277. How does the congregation deal with manifest and impenitent sinners?

Manifest and impenitent sinners must be *excluded from the Christian congregation.*

660 *Put away* from among yourselves that wicked person. *1 Cor.* 5:13.

278. What steps must be taken before a manifest and impenitent sinner is excluded from the congregation?

The Scriptures give us the following directions: "If thy brother shall trespass against thee, go and *tell him his fault between thee and him alone.* If he shall hear thee, thou hast gained thy brother.

"But if he will *not hear thee,* then *take with thee one or two more,* that in the mouth of two or three witnesses every word may be established.

"And *if he shall neglect to hear them, tell it unto the church;* but if he *neglect to hear the church,* let him be unto thee as an *heathen man and a publican.*" (Matt. 18:15-17. Stages of admonition.)

279. What is this act of excluding the manifest and impenitent sinner called?

This act is called *excommunication*.

280. What is the duty of the called minister of Christ when the congregation has excommunicated a sinner?

The called minister of Christ must carry out the resolution of the congregation, that is, he must *exclude the excommunicated sinner from the rights and privileges of a Christian.*

281. How should we regard such action of the congregation?

Such action of the congregation is *as valid and certain*, in heaven also, *as if Christ*, our dear Lord, *acted Himself.*

661 Verily I say unto you, *Whatsoever ye shall bind on earth shall be bound in heaven.* Matt. 18:18.

282. What is the purpose of excommunication?

Excommunication is intended, not for the eternal *ruin* of the excommunicated, but for the *salvation* of his soul. He is to see the greatness of his sin and is to repent.

283. How should the excommunicated person be dealt with when he shows himself penitent?

If he confesses his sin to the congregation and promises to amend, the congregation should *receive him again as a brother.*

662   Sufficient to such a man is this punishment, which was inflicted of many, so that contrariwise ye ought rather to forgive him and comfort him, lest perhaps such a one should be swallowed up with overmuch sorrow. Wherefore I beseech you that ye would *confirm your love toward him.* To whom ye forgive anything, I forgive also; for if I forgave anything, to whom I forgave it, for your sakes forgave I it in the person of Christ. *2 Cor. 2:6-8, 10.*

CONFESSION AND ABSOLUTION

What is Confession? Confession embraces two parts. One is that we confess our sins; the other, that we receive absolution, or forgiveness, from the pastor as from God Himself, and in no wise doubt, but firmly believe, that by it our sins are forgiven before God in heaven.

---

284. What is the first part of Confession?

The first part of Confession is that we *confess,* or acknowledge, *our sins.*

What sins should we confess? Before God we should plead guilty of all sins, even of those which we do not know, as we do in the Lord's Prayer; but before the pastor we should confess those sins only which we know and feel in our hearts.

285. What sins should we confess before God?

Before God we should plead guilty of *all sins*, even of those which we do not know, as we do in the Fifth Petition of the Lord's Prayer and in the General Confession.

663   Who can understand his errors? Cleanse Thou me from *secret faults. Ps. 19:12.*

664   He that *covereth* his sins shall *not prosper;* but whoso *confesseth* and forsaketh them *shall have mercy. Prov. 28:13.*

665   If we say that we have no sin, we deceive ourselves, and the truth is not in us. If we *confess our sins,* He is faithful and just to forgive us our sins and to cleanse us from all unrighteousness. *1 John 1:8, 9.*

286. What sins should we confess before the pastor?

Before the pastor we should confess *those sins only* which we know and feel in our hearts.

THE GENERAL CONFESSION

O almighty God, merciful Father, I, a poor, miserable sinner, confess unto Thee all my sins and iniquities with which I have ever offended Thee and justly deserved Thy temporal and eternal punishment. But I am heartily sorry for them and sincerely repent of them, and I pray Thee of Thy boundless mercy and for the sake of the holy, innocent, bitter sufferings and death of Thy beloved Son, Jesus Christ, to be gracious and merciful to me, a poor sinful being. Amen.

What instruction does Dr. Luther give us for examining ourselves before Confession? Here consider your station according to the Ten Commandments, whether you are a father, mother, son, daughter, master, mistress, servant; whether you have been disobedient, unfaithful, slothful; whether you have grieved any person by word or deed; whether you have stolen, neglected, or wasted aught, or done other injury.

287. What is the second part of Confession?

The second part of Confession is that we *receive absolution,* or the forgiveness of sins.

THE ABSOLUTION

Upon this your confession, I, by virtue of my office, as a called and ordained servant of the Word, announce the grace of God unto all of you, and in the stead and by the command of my Lord Jesus Christ I forgive you all your sins in the name of the Father and of the Son and of the Holy Ghost. Amen.

288. How should we regard the absolution, or forgiveness of sins, pronounced by the pastor?

We should regard the absolution as if pronounced by *God Himself* and in no wise doubt, but *firmly believe,* that by it *our sins are forgiven before God in heaven.*

666   Whosesoever sins ye remit, they *are remitted* unto them. *John 20:23.*

667   Whatsoever ye shall loose on earth *shall be loosed in heaven. Matt. 18:18.*

289. Do hypocrites, that is, people who with their lips confess their sins, but are impenitent at heart, receive the forgiveness of sins?

Hypocrites do *not* receive the forgiveness; for they *do not accept the grace of God* that is offered to them in the absolution.

668   The Word preached *did not profit them, not being mixed with faith* in them that heard it. *Heb. 4:2.*

290. Should a Christian confess his sins to his neighbor whom he has offended and grieved?

Yes; for he who is not willing to do this shows clearly that *also before God he does not repent* of his sins.

669   Confess your faults *one to another. James 5:16.*

670   If thou bring thy gift to the altar and there remem- berest *that thy brother hath aught against thee,* leave there thy gift before the altar and *go thy way; first be reconciled* to thy brother and *then come* and offer thy gift. *Matt. 5:23, 24.*

291. What confession do we have in addition to the public, or general, confession before God?

In addition to the public, or general, con- fession before God we have the *private confession before the pastor.*

292. Must a Christian privately confess his sins before the pastor?

A Christian *should not be forced* to make a private confession before the pastor.

293. Which sins may we confess before the pastor?

Before the pastor we may confess those sins *which we know and feel in our hearts.*

294. What benefit do we derive from making such private confession?

When we confess our sins to our pastor and ask for forgiveness (absolution) of such sins as especially burden our conscience, we receive *the comforting assurance that these sins are forgiven.*

671   Son, be of *good cheer;* thy sins *be forgiven* thee. Matt. 9:2.

672   David said unto Nathan, *I have sinned* against the Lord. And Nathan said unto David, *The Lord also hath put away thy sin;* thou shalt not die. 2 Sam. 12:13.

295. Must I not fear that the pastor to whom I have confessed will tell other people of my sins?

The pastor to whom I have privately confessed my sin must keep such confession *strictly to himself.*

Host and Cup

PART VI

The Sacrament of the Altar

296. By what other names is the Sacrament of the Altar known?

The Sacrament of the Altar is known also as the *Lord's Supper,* the *Lord's Table, Holy Communion,* the *Breaking of Bread,* and the *Eucharist.*

673   When ye come together therefore into one place, this is not to eat the *Lord's Supper. 1 Cor. 11:20.*

674   Ye cannot be partakers of the *Lord's Table* and of the table of devils. *1 Cor. 10:21.*

675   For we, being many, are one bread and *one body;* for we are *all partakers of that one bread. 1 Cor. 10:17.* (Communion.)

Note. — See 1 Cor. 10:16.

676   They continued steadfastly in the Apostles' doctrine and fellowship, and in *breaking of bread,* and in prayers. *Acts 2:42.*

677   When He had *given thanks,* He brake it. *1 Cor. 11:24.* (Eucharist.)

I. WHAT THE LORD'S SUPPER IS

What is the Sacrament of the Altar?
It is the true body and blood of our Lord
Jesus Christ under the bread and wine,
for us Christians to eat and to drink,
instituted by Christ Himself.

Where is this written?   The holy Evangelists Matthew, Mark, Luke, and
St. Paul [the Apostle] write thus:
Our Lord Jesus Christ, the same night in
which He was betrayed, took bread;
and when He had given thanks, He
brake it and gave it to His disciples,
saying, Take, eat; this is My body,
which is given for you.   This do in remembrance of Me.

After the same manner also He took the
cup when He had supped, and when
He had given thanks, He gave it to
them, saying, Drink ye all of it; this cup
is the new testament in My blood,
which is shed for you for the remission
of sins.   This do, as oft as ye drink it,
in remembrance of Me.

NOTE. — Matt. 26:26-28.   Mark 14:22-24.   Luke 22:19, 20.
1 Cor. 11:23-25.

297. Who instituted this Sacrament?

Our Lord Jesus Christ, the *truthful, all-wise,* and *almighty God-man,* has instituted this Sacrament.

678 The Word of the Lord is *right;* and all His works are done in *truth. Ps. 33:4.*

679 Unto Him that is able *to do exceeding abundantly above all that we ask or think,* according to the power that worketh in us, unto Him be glory in the Church. *Eph. 3:20, 21.*

298. What are the visible means (elements) in this Sacrament?

The visible means are *bread,* prepared of flour, and *wine,* the fruit of the vine.

299. What does Christ give us in, with, and under these visible means in the Lord's Supper?

In, with, and under the *bread* Christ gives us His *true body;* in, with, and under the *wine* He gives us His *true blood.* (Real Presence.)

300. Why do you believe in the real presence of Christ's body and blood in the Lord's Supper?

I believe in the real presence —

A. Because Jesus says, "This *is* My body, which is *given for you*"; "This *is* My blood of the new testament, which is *shed for you*" (*Matt. 26: 26, 28; Mark 14:22, 24; Luke 22:19, 20; 1 Cor. 11:24, 25*);

B. Because the Bible states that the cup **is** the *communion* of the blood of Christ and that the bread is the *communion* of the body of Christ;

680 The cup of blessing which we bless, is it not the *communion* of the blood of Christ? The bread which we break, is it not the *communion* of the body of Christ? *1 Cor. 10:16.*

c. Because the Bible states that *unworthy communicants are guilty,* not of the bread and wine, but *of the body and blood of Christ;*

681 Whosoever shall eat this bread and drink this cup of the Lord unworthily shall be guilty of the *body* and *blood* of the Lord. *1 Cor. 11:27.*

d. Because no man has the right to change the meaning of a *divine institution and testament.*

682 This is My blood of the new *testament. Mark 14:24.*

683 Though it be but a *man's covenant,* yet if it be confirmed, no man *disannulleth or addeth thereto. Gal. 3:15.*

301. Are bread and wine changed into the body and blood of Christ?

Bread and wine are *not changed* into the body and blood of Christ; for the Bible expressly declares that *bread and wine are still present in the Sacrament.*

684 As often as ye *eat this bread* and *drink this cup,* ye do show the Lord's death till He come. Wherefore whosoever shall *eat this bread* and *drink this cup* of the Lord unworthily shall be guilty of the body and blood of the Lord. But let a man examine himself, and so let him *eat* of that *bread* and *drink* of that *cup. 1 Cor. 11:26-28.*

685 The *cup* of blessing which we bless, is it not the communion of the blood of Christ? The *bread* which we break, is it not the communion of the body of Christ? *1 Cor. 10:16.*

302. For what use does Christ, our Lord, in, with, and under the bread and wine give us Christians His body and His blood?

Christ gives us Christians His body and His blood *to eat and to drink*.

303. Should all communicants receive also the wine?

All communicants *should receive the wine* as well as the bread, because the Lord said, "Drink *ye all* of it." Matt. 26:27.

686 *They all* drank of it. *Mark 14:23*.

NOTE. — See 684.

304. Are we to adore the bread and the wine in the Sacrament?

We are *not to adore* the bread and the wine; for the Lord has declared that we should *eat* the bread and *drink* the wine.

305. Is the Sacrament to be regarded as an unbloody sacrifice for the sins of the living and the dead?

The idea that the Sacrament is a real, though unbloody, sacrifice for the sins of the living and the dead is *contrary to the Word of God*, which teaches that Christ's *one sacrifice* made full atonement for *all sins*.

687 By one offering He hath *perfected forever them* that are sanctified. . . . Now, where remission of these [sins] is, there is *no more offering* for sin. *Heb. 10:14, 18*.

306. In what manner are bread and wine received by the communicant?

Bread and wine are received by the communicant *like any other food,* in a *natural manner.*

307. How are Christ's body and blood received by the communicant?

Like bread and wine, Christ's body and blood are received by the communicant with *his mouth,* but in a *supernatural manner.*

308. What do we call the eating and drinking of Christ's body and blood in, with, and under the bread and wine?

We call this eating and drinking a *sacramental eating and drinking* because it takes place only *in the Sacrament of the Altar.*

309. What does Christ, our Lord, require when He says, "This do in remembrance of Me"?

When the Lord says, "This do in remembrance of Me," He requires that this Sacrament *should forever be administered* in His Church and that we should *especially remember* and *proclaim His death* when we partake of the Lord's Supper.

688   As often as ye eat this bread and drink this cup, ye do *show the Lord's death* till He come. *1 Cor. 11:26.*

310. When only have we the true Lord's Supper?

We have the true Lord's Supper *only* when we administer it *according to Christ's institution;* for He said, *"This do."*

311. Are we to receive the Lord's Supper but once in our life, as we do Baptism?

We should receive the Lord's Supper *frequently*; for St. Paul says, *"As often as* ye eat this bread and drink this cup."

312. Why should we receive the Lord's Supper frequently?

We should receive the Lord's Supper frequently because —

A. Christ *commands,* or urgently invites us, saying, "This do in remembrance of Me";

689   This do ye, as *oft* as ye drink it, in remembrance of Me. For as *often* as ye eat this bread and drink this cup, ye do show the Lord's death till He come. *1 Cor. 11:25, 26.*

690   They *continued steadfastly* in the Apostles' doctrine and fellowship, and *in breaking of bread*, and in prayers. *Acts 2:42.*

B. Christ *promises* to bestow upon us His blessings, "Given and shed for you for the remission of sins";

691   Come unto Me, all ye that labor and are heavy laden, and I will *give you rest. Matt. 11:28.*

C. *We need* the forgiveness of sins and the strength to resist the devil, the world, and our flesh.

NOTE. — See No. 20 under Christian Questions, page 35.

II. THE BENEFITS
OF THE LORD'S SUPPER

What is the benefit of such eating and drinking? That is shown us by these words, "Given and shed for you for the remission of sins"; namely, that in the Sacrament forgiveness of sins, life, and salvation are given us through these words. For where there is forgiveness of sins, there is also life and salvation.

313. What do these words, "Given and shed for you for the remission of sins," tell us?

These words tell us that in the Sacrament Christ gives to *every* communicant as a *pledge* of the remission of sins that *same body and blood* with which He *earned for us* the forgiveness of sins.

314. What do we receive together with the forgiveness of sins?

"Where there is forgiveness of sins, there is *also life and salvation.*"

315. For what purpose, then, do we approach the Lord's Table?

We approach the Lord's Table —

A. Chiefly to receive forgiveness of our sins and thus to be *strengthened in our faith* in our Lord Jesus Christ;

692 This is My body which is *given for you:* this do in remembrance of Me. . . . This cup is the new testament in My blood, which is *shed for you. Luke 22:19, 20.*

B. To *obtain strength for a holier life;*

693 He died for all, that they which live should *not henceforth live unto themselves, but unto Him* which died for them and rose again. If any man be *in Christ,* he is a new creature. *2 Cor. 5:15, 17.*

c. To bear testimony that we are of one faith with those who commune with us.

NOTE. — See 1 Cor. 10:17; Acts 2:42.

III. THE POWER
OF THE LORD'S SUPPER

How can bodily eating and drinking do such great things? It is not the eating and drinking indeed that does them, but the words here written, "Given and shed for you for the remission of sins"; which words, besides the bodily eating and drinking, are the chief thing in the Sacrament; and he that believes these words has what they say and express, namely, the forgiveness of sins.

---

316. Has eating and drinking the power to impart the forgiveness of sins?

It is *not the eating and drinking* indeed that imparts the forgiveness of sins.

317. How, then, does the Sacrament impart such forgiveness of sins?

By His words "Given and shed for you for the remission of sins" Christ *has placed the forgiveness of sins into the Sacrament,* and there *He offers, gives, and seals* it to all communicants. *These words,* therefore, are the *chief thing* in the Sacrament.

318. How do we receive this benefit?

We receive this benefit *only by believing these words,* "Given and shed for you for the remission of sins."

IV. THE SALUTARY USE
OF THE LORD'S SUPPER

Who, then, receives such Sacrament worthily? Fasting and bodily preparation are indeed a fine outward training; but he is truly worthy and well prepared who has faith in these words, "Given and shed for you for the remission of sins."

But he that does not believe these words, or doubts, is unworthy and unprepared; for the words "for you" require all hearts to believe.

319. Why should we consider the true worthiness of a communicant?

We should consider this because St. Paul expressly instructs us: "Let a man *examine himself*, and so let him eat of that bread and drink of that cup. For he that eateth and drinketh *unworthily*, eateth and drinketh damnation to himself, not discerning the Lord's body," *1 Cor. 11:28, 29.*

320. Is it necessary to fast before partaking of the Sacrament?

Christ *nowhere commands nor forbids* us to fast.

321. Is any other bodily preparation commanded for true worthiness?

No other bodily preparation is commanded for true worthiness; but a proper regard for the Lord's Supper should induce us to appear at the Lord's Table with *modesty and reverence.*

322. In what does true worthiness consist?

True worthiness consists *in faith* in these words, "Given and shed for you for the remission of sins."

323. Who is unworthy and unprepared?

A person who *does not believe* these words, "Given and shed for you for the remission of sins," or *who doubts* these words, is unworthy and unprepared. For the words "for you" require all hearts to believe.

324. How should we examine ourselves before partaking of Communion?

We should examine ourselves to see —

A. Whether we truly *repent* of our sins;

B. Whether we *believe* in Jesus Christ as our Savior;

C. Whether we have the good and earnest purpose with the aid of God the Holy Spirit henceforth to *amend* our sinful lives.

NOTE. — As a preparation for Holy Communion use Christian Questions on pages 31 to 35.

325. May believers whose faith is weak approach the Lord's Table?

Believers whose faith is weak should indeed come to the Lord's Supper *that their faith may grow stronger.*

694   Lord, I believe; *help* Thou mine unbelief. *Mark 9:24.*

695   A *bruised reed* shall He not break, and the *smoking flax* shall He not quench. *Is. 42:3.*

696   Him that cometh to Me I will *in no wise cast out.* *John 6:37.*

326. To whom must the Lord's Supper be denied?

The Lord's Supper must be denied —

A. To those who are known to be *ungodly* and *impenitent;*

697   He that eateth and drinketh *unworthily*, eateth and drinketh *damnation to himself*, not *discerning the Lord's body. 1 Cor. 11:29.*

B. To those who have *given offense* and have not *removed it;*

698 If thou bring thy gift to the altar and there rememberest that thy brother hath aught against thee, leave there thy gift before the altar and go thy way; *first be reconciled* to thy brother, and then come and offer thy gift. *Matt. 5:23, 24.*

C. To those who are *not able to examine themselves,* such as children and adults who have not been sufficiently instructed, and persons who are unconscious;

699 Let a man *examine himself,* and so let him eat of that bread and drink of that cup. *1 Cor. 11:28.*

D. To those of a different faith, since the Lord's Supper is a testimony of the *unity of faith.*

700 They continued steadfastly in the *Apostles' doctrine* and fellowship, and in *breaking of bread,* and in prayers. *Acts 2:42.*

701 I beseech you, brethren, mark them which cause divisions and offenses *contrary to the doctrine* which ye have learned; and *avoid them. Rom. 16:17.* (Close Communion.)

327. What do we ask of all those who wish to commune at our altars?

We ask that they *make* their *intention known to the pastor,* so that he may have opportunity to speak to them in the interest of their spiritual welfare.

328. Whom do we admit to the Lord's Table?

We admit to the Lord's Table those who have received *sufficient instruction* and have given an account of their faith.

329. What custom do we, therefore, observe?

We observe the custom of *confirmation*.

330. What is confirmation?

Confirmation is the rite by which a baptized person renews his baptismal vow, publicly confesses his faith, and is received into communicant membership by the congregation.

331. What should be the prayer of the congregation on the day of confirmation?

On the day of confirmation the congregation should *pray for the catechumens* that they may grow in grace, be steadfast in the profession of their faith, become fruitful in every good work, and in the end receive the crown of life.

702 Be thou *faithful unto death*, and I will give thee a crown of life. *Rev. 2:10.*

703 *Hold* that *fast* which thou hast, that no man take thy crown. *Rev. 3:11.*

APPENDIX

Books of the Bible

The Bible is divided into two parts, the Old Testament and the New Testament. There are sixty-six books in the Bible: thirty-nine in the Old Testament and twenty-seven in the New Testament.

BOOKS OF THE OLD TESTAMENT

Historical Books

Gen'e-sis ⎤
Ex'o-dus ⎥ *The*
Le-vit'i-cus ⎬ *Pen'ta-teuch*
Num'bers ⎥ (Five Books
Deu-ter-on'o-my ⎦ of Moses)

Josh'u-a
Judg'es
Ruth
First Sam'u-el
Second Sam'u-el
First Kings
Second Kings
First Chron'i-cles
Second Chron'i-cles
Ez'ra
Ne-he-mi'ah
Es'ther

Poetical Books

Job
Psalms
Prov'erbs
Ec-cle-si-as'tes
 or The Preacher
Song of Sol'o-mon

Prophetical Books

Major Prophets

I-sa'iah
Jer-e-mi'ah
 Lam-en-ta'tions
E-ze'kiel
Dan'iel

Minor Prophets

Ho-se'a	Na'hum
Jo'el	Hab-ak'kuk
A'mos	Zeph-a-ni'ah
O-ba-di'ah	Hag'gai
Jo'nah	Zech-a-ri'ah
Mi'cah	Mal'a-chi

BOOKS OF THE NEW TESTAMENT

Historical Books

Mat'thew
Mark
Luke
John
The Acts of the Apostles

Epistles

Ro'mans
First Co-rin'thi-ans
Second Co-rin'thi-ans
Ga-la'tians
E-phe'sians
Phi-lip'pi-ans
Co-los'sians
First Thes-sa-lo'nians
Second Thes-sa-lo'nians

First Tim'-o-thy
Second Tim'o-thy
Ti'tus
Phi-le'mon
He'brews
James
First Pe'ter
Second Pe'ter
First John
Second John
Third John
Jude

Prophetical Book

The Revelation of St. John

Our English Bible

The Old Testament was written in Hebrew and the New Testament in Greek. Our English Bible is a translation from the Hebrew and the Greek. The English Bible in ordinary use is called the Authorized Version, or the King James Bible. It is a translation which a body of learned men prepared and published in England in 1611, during the reign of James I.

Creeds and Confessions

Our Lutheran Church has nine creeds and confessions in which we state what we believe.

The Ecumenical (or Universal) Creeds are:

1. The Apostles' Creed.
2. The Nicene Creed.
3. The Athanasian Creed.

The Confessions of the Evangelical Lutheran Church are:

1. The Augsburg Confession.
2. The Apology of the Augsburg Confession.
3. The Smalcald Articles.
4. The Small Catechism of Luther.
5. The Large Catechism of Luther.
6. The Formula of Concord.

These six Confessions and the Ecumenical Creeds form the Book of Concord, first published in 1580.

The Church Year

The church year has been arranged to set before us the principal events in the Savior's life. The order is as follows:

Four Sundays in Advent.

Christmas.

Festival of Circumcision (January 1).

Epiphany (January 6).

From one to six Sundays after Epiphany (depending on the date of Easter).

Three Sundays before Lent: Septuagesima, Sexagesima, Quinquagesima.

Ash Wednesday (beginning of Lent).

Six Sundays in Lent (the sixth being Palm Sunday).

Holy Week, the week before Easter (including Holy Thursday, or Maundy Thursday, and Good Friday).

Easter.

Five Sundays after Easter.

Ascension Day (40 days after Easter).

Sunday after Ascension.

Pentecost, or Whitsunday (50 days after Easter).

Trinity Sunday (and from 22 to 27 Sundays after Trinity).

The Lutheran Church observes also the Festival of the Reformation on October 31.

Each Sunday and each festival day has its own Gospel and Epistle for the day.

A Short Form for Holy Baptism in Cases of Necessity

In urgent cases, in the absence of the pastor, any Christian may administer Holy Baptism.

Take water, call the child by name, pour or sprinkle the water on the head of the child, saying:

I baptize thee in the name of the Father and of the Son and of the Holy Ghost. Amen.

If there is time, the baptism may be preceded by the following prayer and the Lord's Prayer:

Eternal, merciful God, we pray Thee to extend Thy goodness and mercy unto this child, who now asks; open the door to him (her) who knocks, that he (she) may enjoy the everlasting blessing of Thy heavenly washing and may come to the eternal kingdom which Thou hast prepared through Christ, our Lord. Amen.

Our Father who art in heaven, Hallowed be Thy name; Thy kingdom come; Thy will be done on earth as it is in heaven; Give us this day our daily bread; And forgive us our trespasses, as we forgive those who trespass against us; And lead us not into temptation; But deliver us from evil; For Thine is the kingdom and the power and the glory forever and ever. Amen.

Index of Topics
and
Dictionary of Terms

The references are to the question numbers.

Where the definition of a term is not given, reference may be made to a definition given in the Catechism, thus: CATECHISM. *Def.*, 2.

Root meanings of some terms are printed in italics.

ABSOLUTION. The act of *loosening* or *setting free* from sin and its penalty; forgiveness. 287–289, 267, 271, 294. Certainty of, 276, 288.

ADORATION. Of bread and wine, 304. Of saints, 202 (Is. 63:16).

ADULTERY. Unfaithfulness in marriage; any impurity or unchastity. 62.

ALTAR. A *table*.

AMEN. Certainly; truly; so it is; so shall it be.

ANGEL. 108–111.

ANOINTED ONE, THE. Christ. 123, 132.

APOSTLE. *One sent forth* personally by Christ to preach the Gospel. 8.

APOSTLES' CREED. *Def.*, 102. 100–200.

ATONEMENT. The *setting-at-one*, or reunion, of offended God and sinful mankind, earned by Christ's obedience unto death; reconciliation. 99, 129, 130, 140–147, 152 C, 190, 305.

ATTRIBUTE. Anything that can be said about a person or thing. Of God, 25. Of Christ, 126 B. Of the Holy Ghost, 162 B. Communication of Attributes, 134, 148.

BAPTISM, HOLY. *Def.*, 244, 245. 244–266. Administration of, 247. Adult, 249, 250 A. Benefit of, 253–256. Emergency, 247. Infant, 249–252. Institution of, 246. Power of, 257, 258. Significance of, 259–266. Sponsors, 252.

BELIEF. BELIEVE. BELIEVER. *See* Faith.

BIBLE. The *Book* of God's Word revealed to man; the Book of books. 6–17, 24 C, pages 209, 210. *See* Word of God.

BLASPHEMY. (*Evil-speaking.*) Evil or profane speaking of God. 38 A, 220 B (*Rom. 2: 23, 24*).

BLESSINGS. Bodily or material, 117, 204, 205, 218. Spiritual, 204, 205, 218.

CALL OF HOLY GHOST. *Def.*, 165. 166, 172.

CALLED MINISTER. The minister called, or elected, by a congregation to be its spiritual *servant*. 247, 275, 276, 280.

CARNAL. *Fleshly,* sinful and corrupt, worldly. 95 (*Rom. 8:7*).

CATECHISM. *Def.,* 2. 1—4.

CATHOLIC. *Def.,* 179, *Note.*

CHARITY. Christian *love* of one's fellow men. 21, 52—54, 60, 67 C, 69 C, 73.

CHASTITY. *Pureness,* decency, modesty, 63, 64.

CHRIST. The title, 123. The name Jesus, 122. Ascension, 153. Birth, 137. Blood, 145, 299—302, 313. Body, 127 B, 177, 299—302, 313. Burial, 139. Conception, 136. Death, 129 B, 130 B, 138 C, 145, 254. Descent into hell, 150. Divinity (Deity), 26, 27, 125, 126, 130, 152 A. Exaltation, 148—156. Faith in, *see* Faith. Foundation of Church, 179. Head of Church, 177. Humanity, 125, 127—129. Humiliation, 134—139. Instituted Sacraments, 246, 297. Natures, 125—131. Obedience of, 132. Office as King, Priest, Prophet, 132, 155. Resurrection, 151, 152, 158. Return to judge, 156. Saving knowledge of, 166. Sitting on right hand of God, 154, 155. States, 133. Suffering, 129 B, 138, 145, 254. Union of natures, 128.

CHRISTIAN. *Belonging to Christ;* believing in Christ; pertaining to Christ or His religion. 179.

CHURCH. (*Belonging to the Lord.*)
a. The Holy Christian, or Invisible, *def.,* 175. 172, 175—186.
b. The Visible, *def.,* 182.
c. The Local, *def.,* 185.
d. Denomination, *def.,* 183, 184.
e. Church building, 181 D.

CHURCH DISCIPLINE. *See* Office of Keys.

CHURCH YEAR. Page 211.

CLOSE COMMUNION. 326.

COMFORTER. The Holy Spirit, who *comforts* with faith in the forgiveness of sins, 166, 194 C.

COMMANDMENTS, THE TEN. *See* Law.

COMMUNE. To partake of Holy Communion.

COMMUNICANT.
a. One who takes Communion. Worthy, unworthy, 300 C, 319—326.
b. A member entitled to Communion. 328, 330.

COMMUNICATE. To *share,* give, 51 C (*Gal. 6:6*). Also, to give Holy Communion.

COMMUNICATION OF ATTRIBUTES. 134, 148.

COMMUNION. Of elements, 299—301. Of natures, 128.

COMMUNION, HOLY. *See* Lord's Supper.

COMMUNION OF SAINTS. The *union* in Christ of all those who by faith in Him are *holy* in God's sight; the Church Invisible. 175—186.

CONFESSION. The *telling* or admitting of sin and guilt, with the receiving of forgiveness from the pastor. 284–295. General, 285, 289. Private, 291–295. *See* p. 210.

CONFIDENCE. Of faith, 103. In prayer, 206, 208.

CONFIRMATION. CONFIRM. (*Make firm.*) *Def.*, 330. 329–331.

CONGREGATION. (*Flock.*) *Def.*, 185. Has power of keys, 270, 275, 277–283.

CONSCIENCE. The personal sense or feeling of being right or wrong. Testifies of God, 24 B. Troubled, 293, 294.

CONTRITION. (*A being crushed.*) Deep sorrow for sin; terror of conscience. 260, 272.

CONVERSION. CONVERT. God's *turning* man from sin and unbelief to faith in Christ. 166, 167.

CORRUPTION. State of decay and impurity; depravity. *See* Original Sin.

COVET. COVETOUSNESS. (*Eager desire.*) 70, 71, 74, 75, 78.

CREATION. *Def.*, 106, 107. 27. Of man, 112, 115.

CREED. (Latin: *Credo – I believe.*) 100. *See* also p. 210.

CURSING. *Def.*, 38.

DAMNATION. The everlasting punishment in hell; eternal death. 78, 80, 196 B.

DEATH.
  a. Temporal, bodily death: separation of soul from body at the end of life. 80. Of Christ, *see* Christ.

  b. Spiritual death: separation of the soul from God by unbelief. 164.

  c. Eternal death: separation of soul and body from God in the unending agony of hell. 196 B. Redemption from, 143.

DENOMINATION. *See* Church.

DEVIL. An evil angel; especially, the *false accuser*, Satan, the personal chief of the devils. 92, 111, 130 B, 144, 226, 227, 238, 264, 312 C.

DIVINE. *Of God;* like God; God's.

DIVINITY. DEITY. Of Christ, *see* Christ. Of Holy Ghost, 26, 27, 161, 162.

DIVORCE. The public, legal declaration that the marriage tie has been broken. 62.

DOCTRINE. That which is taught; a *teaching.* Christian, 4–6, 102, 219, 250. False, 43, 220.

ELECTION OF GRACE. Predestination. 199.

ELEMENTS. *See* Means.

EMERGENCY BAPTISM. 247. *For form to be used, see* p. 212.

ENLIGHTENMENT. *Def.*, 166.

EUCHARIST. (*Giving thanks.*) The Lord's Supper. 296.

EVANGELICAL. Pertaining to the Evangel, or *Gospel.*

EVANGELICAL LUTHERAN CHURCH. The Church which follows *Luther* in teaching the *Gospel* of God's Word in all the purity which he restored.

EVANGELIST. (*Bringer of good news.*) A writer of one of the four Gospels. 8.

EVOLUTION, THEORY OF. The idea that all things have evolved, or developed, in the course of long ages, from simple forms to more complex forms. This theory contradicts the Bible account of the creation.

EXALTATION OF CHRIST. (*Raising very high.*) 148—156.

EXCOMMUNICATION. (*Putting out of union.*) 277—283.

FAITH. *Def.*, 103. Faith in Christ, *def.*, 124, 166. 12, 163, 168, 272. Impossible without Holy Ghost, 164, who calls to faith, 165, works it, 163, 166, 223, 260, by the means of grace, 168, 242, 254, 258, 315, and preserves in it, 171, 172, 227. Must be personal, 104. Necessary for benefit of Baptism, 255, and of Lord's Supper, 318. Makes up true worthiness, 322. Is strengthened, 236, in Lord's Supper, 315, 325. Accepts forgiveness, 168, 192, 257, 288, 318. Receives eternal life, 196—199. Saves without Baptism, 256. Lack of, makes unworthy, 319, 323, and damns, 196, 255, 256. In prayer, 206, 208. Tested, 236, 239. Unity of, 177, 315 C, 326 D. The Church and, 175, 182, 186 A. Fruits of, 169, 170, 261—263, 315 B.

FALL OF MAN. 88, 92, 114.

FASTING. Not commanded, 320.

FATHERHOOD OF GOD. 105, 215, 216.

FEAR OF GOD. 31, 34, 83.

FLESH. The material part of man; hence, man's inability to do good, the completely spoiled condition of his entire nature since the Fall. 226, 227, 238, 312 C.

FORGIVENESS. 187—194, 231—234, 267—295. Certainty of, 193. For Christ's sake, 145, 146, 189, 231. Faith accepts and receives, 168, 192, 257, 288, 318. Importance of doctrine of, 194. Of neighbor, 60, 233, 234. Obtained for all, 190. Offered in Gospel, 191, and in Sacraments, 242, 257, 317. Offered and given by minister, 276, 288, 294. Pledged in Lord's Supper, 313. Wrought by Baptism, 253.

GENTILE. A non-Jew. A heathen.

GOD. His attributes, 25. Existence, 24. Love, *see* Grace. Right hand, 154. Unity and Trinity, 26. Alone to be prayed to, 202. *See* Fatherhood; Christ; Holy Ghost.

GOOD WORKS. *See* Works, Good.

GOSPEL. (*Good news.*) *Def.*, 16. 14, 99. Differs from Law, 17. Is means of grace, 168, 191. Is mark of Church, 180. Works faith, 165, 168.

GOVERNMENT. Of God, 117. Of Christ, 132 C, 154, 155 C. Of men, 55—57.

GRACE OF GOD. The love and favor of God toward undeserving man. 25. Moves Him to forgive, 189, 231. Offered, 289. Promised for obedience, 84.

HEAVEN. The final condition and place of eternal bliss in the presence of God and the angels. 196, 197. Opened or closed, 268. Office of Keys valid in, 276, 281.

HELL. The final condition and place of the unbelievers and evil angels condemned by God to eternal punishment. 150, 196.

HOLY COMMUNION. *See* Lord's Supper.

HOLY GHOST. HOLY SPIRIT. 10, 26, 27, 123, 136, 161—174, 176 B, 254, 258.

HUMILIATION OF CHRIST. 134—140.

HYPOCRITE. One who only *pretends* to be a believer. 43, 182, 289.

IDOLATRY. (*Idol service.*) 28, 29.

IMAGE OF GOD. 112—114.

IMMERSION. (*Dipping in.*) 244.

IMMORTAL. *Undying;* not subject to death. 197.

IMPENITENT SINNER. 274, 277—280, 326.

IMPUTE. To *charge with* sin or guilt; to *credit with* righteousness. 188.

INCARNATION. The taking on of a human body and soul by the Son of God, so that He is now both God and man in one undivided person. 125, 127—129, 136, 137.

INFANT BAPTISM. 249—252.

INHERITED SIN. 93—97.

INIQUITY. (*Unevenness, unequalness.*) That which does not measure up to the requirements of God's Law; sin. *See* Sin.

INSPIRATION. (*Breathing into.*) 9—11.

INTERCEDE. INTERCESSION. (*Pass between.*) Beg or plead in behalf of others. Of Christ, 132 B, 155 B.

JEALOUS. Demanding all honor and glory for Himself, and *permitting no rivals.* 79.

JESUS. The name, 122. *See* Christ.

JUDGMENT, THE LAST. 156.

JUST. *Lawful, right,* righteous, guiltless.

JUSTIFICATION. *Def.,* 188. 187—194.

KINGDOM. Of Christ, 132 C, 154, 155 C, 157 B. Of God, 117 B, 222, 223, 241. *See* Church.

KNOWLEDGE. Required for faith, 103. Of God, 24, 113 A. Of Jesus, a gift, 166.

LAW. *Def.,* 15. 14, 18—23. Differs from Gospel, 17. Perfect fulfillment demanded, 87, 88. No salvation by it, 89. Purpose, 90. Fulfilled by Christ, 99, 130 A, 132 B. Tables of, 19—21. Ten Commandments of, 24—86, 170.

LIFE. Eternal, 152 D, 197—199. Spiritual, 258, 261, 314.

LORD'S PRAYER. 213—241. *See* Prayer.

LORD'S SUPPER. *Def.,* 296. 297—331. Announcement for, 327. Institution, 297. Real Presence, 299—301, 307, 308, 313. Proper use of, 302—310. Frequent use of, 311, 312. Benefits of, 313—315. Power of, 316—318. Salutary use of, 319—328.

218

INDEX AND DICTIONARY

LOVE. Of God, *see* Grace. Of man, toward creatures, 29; toward God, 20, 30, 32, 78, 86; toward neighbor, 21, 52—54. In marriage, 65. Is Summary of Commandments, 22.

LUST, EVIL. Sinful desire, 78.

LUTHER, DR. MARTIN. 3, 4, 6. Born, A. D. 1483; published Ninety-five Theses, 1517; wrote Catechism, 1529; translated Bible, 1521—1534; died, 1546.

MAN. 112—115. Lost by own fault, 173, 174. Image of God in, 112—114.

MANIFEST. Plain, easily seen, unmistakable. Sinner, 277—279.

MARRIAGE. *Def.*, 61. 62, 65.

MEANS, EXTERNAL OR VISIBLE. 242, 244, 298, 299, 301.

MEANS OF GRACE. The *instruments* or channels through which God offers and gives the grace of His forgiveness — the Gospel and the Sacraments. 168, 191, 254, 276, 315.

MERIT. That which *deserves* reward or earns payment; worth. None in man, 118, 189.

MESSIAH. The *Anointed* One. 123.

MILLENNIUM. (A *1,000-year* period.) A long period before the end of the world, during which the believers are supposed to enjoy outward peace, prosperity, and power. There is no foundation for this belief in the Bible. 195—197.

MINISTER. The pastor as *servant* of Christ and His Church. To baptize, 247. Deals in name of God and of congregation, 275, 276, 280.

MINISTRY, OFFICE OF. 51 C. See Minister.

MIRACLE. A *wonder* or very unusual happening brought about by God without regard to the natural order of things. 126 C, 136.

MISSIONS. (*Send.*) 51 D, 186 C, 223 B.

MORTAL. Subject to *death*.

NAME OF GOD. *Def.*, 35. 219—221. Abuse of, 36—43. Proper use of, 44. In Baptism, 245, 248. Name of Jesus in prayer, 206.

NATURAL MAN. Man as he is by *birth* before conversion. And the Law, 88, 94—96. And faith in Christ, 164.

NEIGHBOR. 21, 52—54, 170, 229, 234, 290.

NEW BIRTH. *See* Regeneration.

NEW MAN. 114, 167—169, 261—263.

OBEDIENCE. Of Christ, 132. To parents and superiors, 57. To God, 79, 84—88, 119.

OFFEND. GIVE OFFENSE. Not, to hurt a person's feelings, but to harm his faith, to *cause him to stumble or fall* into sin by anything we teach or do. 251 C (*Matt. 18:6*), 326 B.

OFFICE. The right to exercise a power, especially publicly. Of Christ, 132. Of Keys, 267—295. Of Ministry, 51 C, 275, 276.

OLD ADAM. OLD MAN. 94–97, 259, 260, 263.

ORIGINAL SIN. (*Sin from the beginning.*) 93–97.

PASSION OF CHRIST. The final great *suffering* of Christ. 138.

PASTOR. The minister as *shepherd* of his flock.

PECULIAR. *One's own to have and to use;* special, unique. 269.

PENITENT SINNER. 194 C, 271, 272.

PERJURY. False swearing; swearing to that which is not true. 41.

PERSONAL UNION. 128.

PERSONS IN GOD. 26, 27, 161.

PETITION. An *asking* for something. 201, 214.

PRAYER. *Def.*, 201. In general, 44, 201–212. An aid to chastity, 64. For neighbor, 210, 229. *See* Lord's Prayer.

PREDESTINATION. Election, 199.

PRESERVATION. Of all things, 116, 117. Of faith, 171, 172, 227, 239.

PROMISE OF GOD. In Baptism, 245, 255, 257. In Fourth Commandment, 58. For all Commandments, 84–86. Is sure, 193. Should move, to pray, 203, and to commune often, 312.

PROPHET. (*Speak for another.*) One through whom God makes known His will to man. 8. Christ our, 132, 155.

PROPITIATION. (*Making favorable.*) That which satisfies God's just demands, removes His wrath, and earns His favor — Christ's atoning sacrifice. 142, 145–147, 190.

PROVIDENCE OF GOD. God's preservation and government of the universe by His power for His own good and wise purposes. 116, 117.

PUBLICAN. Tax collector for the Roman Empire, usually dishonest and wicked.

PURGATORY. (*Purge, cleanse.*) According to the teaching of the Roman Catholic Church, a state, or condition, in which, after death, souls are purified for their entrance into heaven. Scripture speaks only of heaven and hell. 196 B, 197 A.

REAL PRESENCE. 299–301, 307, 308, 313.

RECONCILIATION. (*A bringing together again.*) *See* Atonement.

REDEEM. REDEMPTION. (*Buy back.*) The freeing of mankind from sin, death, and the power of the devil through the blood of Christ, the Redeemer. 27, 130 B, 140–147. Purpose of, 157. Certainty of, 158.

REGENERATION. (*Rebirth.*) 166, 167. In Baptism, 251, 258, 261.

REMEMBRANCE. Of Christ in Lord's Supper, 309.

REMIT. REMISSION. To forgive. 267, 268, 271. *See* Forgiveness.

RENEWAL. Sanctification (in the narrower sense). 169. In Baptism, 258, 261–263.

REPENTANCE. 260, 263, 273, 282, 290, 324.

RESURRECTION. (*Rising again.*) Of Christ, 151, 152. Of the body, 152 D, 195, 196.

RETAIN SIN. To *hold* the person to be still guilty of sin; to refuse forgiveness. 267, 268, 274.

REVELATION. (*Unveiling.*) God's making known what was before unknown. 7, 24 C, 43, 132 A.

RIGHTEOUSNESS. The perfect obedience of Christ, also as credited to the believer. 132 B, 157, 188. None in man by nature, 95.

SABBATH DAY. (*Rest from labor.*) The seventh day of the week (Saturday), the divinely appointed day of rest and worship for Israel. 45.

SACRAMENT. *Def.*, 242, 243. *See* Baptism; Lord's Supper. Administration of, 247, 267, 276, 309, 310. Institution of, 246, 297, 300. Means of grace, 168, 191. In the true Church, 184.

SACRIFICE OF CHRIST. 132 B, 152 C, 305.

SAINT. (*One made holy.*)
a. One who is holy in God's sight by faith in Christ; a believer. 175, 177, 178.
b. A departed believer.

SALUTARY. Giving *safety, health,* and salvation. Use of Lord's Supper, 319–328.

SALVATION. The condition of being *saved* from sin and eternal death. Brought by Christ, 99, 124, 140–147.

Offered and given through the means of grace, 12, 168, 253–255, 257, 314. Certainty of, 158, 193, 199.

SANCTIFICATION. (*Making holy.*) In narrower sense, 169, 170. In wider sense, 163–174. Is work of Holy Ghost, 27, 163, 164, 169.

SAVIOR. 32, 122, 124. *See* Christ.

SCRIPTURE. (*Writing.*) *See* Bible, Word of God.

SEAL. That which makes sure, assures. Said of the Sacraments, 242.

SIN. 91–99. To be confessed, before God, 285, to the neighbor, 290, and to the pastor, 291–295. Forgiven and retained, *see* Forgiveness; Office of Keys. Salvation from, 99, 142 B. Sorrow for, 260, 272, 274. Original, 93–97. Actual, 93, 98. Of commission, of omission, 98. Recognized through God's Law, 19, 90 B.

SPIRIT. *Def.*, 25. 108–111. The Holy, *see* Holy Ghost.

SPIRITUAL. Blessings, 204, 205, 218. Blindness, 164. Life, 258, 261, 314.

SPONSOR. (*Promise solemnly.*) The person who makes the required professions and promises in the name of an infant presented for Baptism. 252.

STATE. Of Exaltation, 148–156. Of Humiliation, 134–139.

SUBSTITUTE. One put in place of another. Christ our, 99, 129–132, 146.

SUFFERING. 225, 227. Of Christ, 138.

SUICIDE. (*Self-killing.*) 59.

SUNDAY. 46, 47.

SWEARING. 37, 39—41.

TEMPERANCE. Moderation in the use of intoxicants. An aid to chastity, 64.

TEMPT. TEMPTATION. (*Test, try.*) 235. To evil, 92, 144, 237—239. To good, 236, 239.

TESTAMENT. A *last will;* a covenant-agreement. Of Bible, 8, 123. Of Christ, 300 D.

THOUGHT. Evil, is sin. 78, 98.

TRANSGRESS. To *step over* the limits of right conduct laid down by God in His Law; sin; trespass. *See* Sin.

TRESPASS. (*To pass over.*) *See* Sin.

TRINITY. TRIUNE. (*Three-in-One.*) 26, 27, 161. In Baptism, 245, 248.

TRUST. Required for faith, 103. In God, 33, 86. In Christ, 166. In creatures, 29.

UNBELIEF. UNBELIEVERS. 174, 196 B, 256, 274, 323, 326.

UNBLOODY SACRIFICE. 305.

UNION. *See* Personal Union.

UNIONISM. Joint worship and church work of those not united in doctrine. 186 D.

VALID. (*Strong.*) Having legal strength or force; that cannot be overthrown or set aside. 276, 281.

VERBAL INSPIRATION. *See* Inspiration.

VICARIOUS. (*One person for another.*) Done by a substitute, said of the atoning sacrifice of Christ in the place of all men. 146.

VOW. A solemn promise made to God. Of Baptism, 265. Renewed, 266, 330.

WASHING OF REGENERATION. 258, 261.

WILL OF GOD. 224—227.

WORD OF GOD. 8, 43, 48—51, 219, 220, 227, 267. In true Church, 184. Connected with visible means, 242. In Baptism, 257. An aid to chastity, 64. *See* Bible.

WORKS, GOOD. *Def.*, 170. 169. Cannot earn forgiveness and salvation, 194 B.

WORLD. 226, 227, 238, 312 C.

WORSHIP. To pay divine honors to; to perform religious exercises in honor of. Of creatures, 29. Public, 45—51, 185. Prayer in, 211.

WORTHINESS. None in man, 118, 189, 232. For Lord's Supper, 319, 328.